Global Challenges and the Emerging World Order

Giulio Sapelli

Global Challenges and the Emerging World Order

 Springer

Giulio Sapelli
University of Milan and Fondazione Eni
   Enrico Mattei (FEEM)
Milan
Italy

Translated from Italian language edition Published by Guerrini e Associati: "Dove va il mondo?"
© 2014 Translation by Juliet Haydock.
Footnotes by Barbara Racah.

ISBN 978-3-319-15623-1   ISBN 978-3-319-15624-8   (eBook)
DOI 10.1007/978-3-319-15624-8

Library of Congress Control Number: 2015933830

Springer Cham Heidelberg New York Dordrecht London
© Springer International Publishing Switzerland 2015
This work is subject to copyright. All rights are reserved by the Publisher, whether the whole or part of the material is concerned, specifically the rights of translation, reprinting, reuse of illustrations, recitation, broadcasting, reproduction on microfilms or in any other physical way, and transmission or information storage and retrieval, electronic adaptation, computer software, or by similar or dissimilar methodology now known or hereafter developed.
The use of general descriptive names, registered names, trademarks, service marks, etc. in this publication does not imply, even in the absence of a specific statement, that such names are exempt from the relevant protective laws and regulations and therefore free for general use.
The publisher, the authors and the editors are safe to assume that the advice and information in this book are believed to be true and accurate at the date of publication. Neither the publisher nor the authors or the editors give a warranty, express or implied, with respect to the material contained herein or for any errors or omissions that may have been made.

Printed on acid-free paper

Springer International Publishing AG Switzerland is part of Springer Science+Business Media (www.springer.com)

Foolery, sir, does walk about the orb like the sun, it shines everywhere.

William Shakespeare, *Twelfth Night*

Acknowledgments

This perhaps somewhat over-ambitious reflection owes much to a think tank that has grown up in a cultural and spiritual setting that is extremely unusual in Italy: the Fondazione Eni Enrico Mattei. It naturally reflects my own thoughts and not those of the Foundation, though without the decision taken by the Foundation Board of Directors to begin work on a new research programme ("Economy and society"), which I led for a few months during its start-up, this book would never have seen the light of day. I am therefore grateful to Paolo Scaroni, President of the Foundation and Giuseppe Sammarco, its Director, who have given me their unflagging trust and encouragement. I would nevertheless certainly not have written these pages had it not been for the decisive encouragement that Joaquín Navarro Valls, who read the first draft of the programme, gave me to expand it into a much longer essay. Luca Farinola was the first to read the work and gave me inestimable advice, as did Daniele Atzori with his great scientific experience, not only in the world of Islam. Filippo Tessari never stopped encouraging me and sharing my view of the programme's direction.

Some short articles exploring these ideas have already appeared in the columns of "Credito Popolare", revealing how much these reflections also owe to my friendship with Giuseppe De Lucia Lumeno. I know that Lodovico Festa, friend and unequalled master of social and political analysis will, in his infinite wisdom, beam down benevolently on the development of thoughts that owe so much to our interminable life-long debates.

Contents

The Terrible August of 2013 1
Start of the Mediterranean Crisis 19
World Economic Crisis 21
The Chickens Have Come Home to Roost 23
The Old and the New Convergence 37
Responding to Strategic Divergences 43
The Challenge to Fossil Fuels and the Crushing
of Convergent Growth 51
The Future Will Be African 57
Emerge from the Crisis in Europe: Change Europe 69

The Terrible August of 2013

The end of August 2013 will go down in the annals of history as an exceptional period, marking as it did a shift in the relationship between great world powers. For the first time in two centuries, the United Kingdom split from the United States over one of the crucial points of the great cultural downward spiral that has taken place in international relations over the last 20 years. I refer to the 20 years that followed in the wake of the Kissinger era after the fall of the USSR. General evidence of the theoretical and practical change came in the shape of the Balkan wars, which marked the transition from theory to practice of the end of the Westphalian period, when in salient areas of geostrategic interests, each nation was free to choose the political system it wanted, though the choosing was done by a handful of bloodthirsty dictators, and any sacrifices could be ruthlessly made. Only areas of the world deemed irrelevant to the world balance could deploy their not-so-secret Westphalian troops in local and intelligence struggles to maintain the balance of terror: Che Guevara in the Congo and Colonel Taylor in Sierra Leone behaved like the fictional characters in Le Carré's novels.

Then came the unhappy period of humanitarian intervention, the way was paved for this back during the Westphalian period. Arming the Mujahideen and the Taliban against the USSR and, once the USSR was defeated, not worrying about whether the Mujahideen and the Taliban dominated the country or whether the Pakistani secret services (ISI) became the true arbiters of relations between the USA and India: all this could only lay the foundations for long-term instability in extremely sensitive areas of the world balance, which were thus always in danger.

The real moment of change came with the Balkan wars between the Southern Slavs. During the early years of the twentieth century, they lit the fuse for World War I, and 20 years ago, during the break-up of Yugoslavia, they again brought humanity face to face with the terrible problem of genocide. Then, the genocide turned into an intra-ethnic struggle within a geographical entity that was no longer a state that spawned nations whose idea of defining their mutual state boundaries was to massacre one another and wipe one another out. This meant that the nation-building was also a humanitarian action against the genocide, performed by different stakeholders: NATO, the USA, Italy, as an agent of the USA (D'Alema government[1]) without the united Europe showing the slightest flicker of life. The link between the United Kingdom and the USA was forged again from that time around the theory that united west and east Coast followers of Leo Strauss (the Neo-Cons), Blairite theorists of the London School of Economics and followers of the great French international legal and constitutional expert Alfred Dumas. Kissinger became an anachronism, Westphalia, a word to forget and the just war was entrusted as and when deemed necessary to the prevailing balance of power in order to justify the divvying up of the world as well as the struggle against international terrorism.

The link between the UK and USA became necessary in order to maintain a transatlantic relationship between Europe and the USA at a time when Germany and Spain were refusing to shed the blood of their soldiers in Afghanistan and Iraq. France recently attempted a rapprochement with the USA during the wars in North Africa. This is what the Arab Spring uprisings really are: wars between the fault lines created by divisions between Sunnis and Shiites and deep internal rifts in the Sunni world that, due to clumsy US intervention, have consolidated as Gulf and North African wars that refer back to state authorities, namely Iraq and Iran for the Shiites and Saudi Arabia for the Sunnis. Egypt, the Germany of North Africa, has never needed states of reference.

This is clear from the age of the Mamluks during the Ottoman Empire, it is clear from the Napoleonic campaigns that—and this is no coincidence—took place in Egypt and nowhere else and it is clear from the Suez crisis of 1956 at the time of Nasser. The only one person to whom it was not clear was President Obama, who mistook the Muslim Brotherhood, cosmopolitan by definition, just like the former Caliphate, for guardians capable of leading a secular nation like Egypt (Abdel-Malik and his seminal book of the 1960s has a lot to teach us on this subject).

---

[1]Following the collapse of Romano Prodi's government, Massimo D'Alema became Italian premier from 1998 until 2000.

And so it was that all the chickens finally came home to roost that August, and everyone seemed to lose the plot. The French forgot that the Sykes-Picot agreement of 1916 gave rise to what was, along with Egypt, the most powerful point of balance in those areas after World War I. In other words, Syria and its relationship with Lebanon and after 1917 with Israel, which despite all the terrible conflicts and wars from Yom Kippur on, clung on miraculously due to the role that the Alawites (Assad's family is Alawite) guaranteed to Syria for approximately 100 years.

The very term "Alawite", denoting an ethnic and religious group with arcane roots whose origin is still the subject of debate, was coined by the French. The French themselves, acting according to the principle of divide and rule, encouraged Alawite aspirations after World War I with the aim of undermining the Arab nationalist plan of the Sunni Muslims. Now France has forgotten its own glorious colonial past and in its desire to take over the UK's relationship with the USA—Hollande is continuing the work of Sarkozy—wishes to wage war on the historical allies that France itself helped to create. The three-way relationship that has come about between Russia (which supports Syria and Iran), Israel and Saudi Arabia, enemy of the Shiites and Alawites, which challenges the age-old enmity against the Shiiites to benefit the stability of the region, guaranteed by the Alawites (Shiites), is therefore at risk of shattering. Only the weight of American and British soldiers and intelligence, along with the French and Italians of course, could halt the intervention in Syria.

Instead, Russia turned the tables on everyone by making an exceptional diplomatic gambit that marked its irreversible return to the Mediterranean. With an agreement worthy of the great school of Ponomarev and Gromyko, the Russian Foreign Minister Lavrov persuaded the UN to issue Resolution 2118 of 27 September 2013, providing a watertight legal framework for a Russian–North American plan to dismantle Syrian chemical weapons. This plan effectively prevented any military intervention, saved Syria from foreign invasion and allowed Assad to remain in power.

But this meant risking leaving the USA dramatically isolated within the international arena at a time when China was becoming increasingly aggressive. The French, naturally unaware of the immense dangers of this isolation, went on to apply even more pressure on Africa as well as a world on the brink of chaos through its proposal—formulated in unorthodox fashion by the French Foreign Minister Laurent Fabius in an article published in *Le Monde* on 5 October 2013—to effectively dismantle the Security Council's power of veto amidst the storms triggered by humanitarian problems, transferring decision-making powers to the

General Assembly. In this way, the principle of the majority would be applied to international order and it would result in chaos, which is what typically happens when democracy is applied on an international scale through a roll-call of states. The principle of power would no longer apply.

This sign of weakness by the USA had an immediate impact in Asia. These effects were compounded by the ongoing division in the USA between Democrats and Republicans over the problem of the ceiling to be applied to public debt and the struggle to prevent the application of the new health laws. The federal state is always on the brink of breaking down whenever such events occur. Obama had to forego the Asian trips that would have laid the ground for the Trans-Pacific Pact. This has already had dramatic effects, particularly on countries that are still unsure of their strategic stance (examples include Indonesia and Myanmar): China opened a bank for financing infrastructures in Jakarta, a bank that competes directly with the Asian Development Bank, traditionally dominated by Japan and the USA. In Asia, the only possible solution to the threatening and bellicose Chinese dominion is firstly to rearm Japan and then surround that country with a crown of armed and developed states. This set-up is naturally bound to challenge China, which is responding aggressively on the basis of the age-old disputes at its borders and spheres of influence of the South China Sea, leading to inevitable dissuasive action by North America.

In North and Central Africa, there does not appear to be any solution: Europe is divided and the French only huff and puff about the imperial culture without the means of doing anything about it. It therefore was and is essential that the USA should continue to maintain its relationship with the United Kingdom, which symbolically as well as militarily represents the only ally that it is able to bring to the table in the chaotic system of international relations. Against this backdrop, the intelligence communities of the United Kingdom and the United States, and particularly the military élites, are extremely opposed to any intervention in Syria because they are aware that the domino effect of such action would reach throughout North and Central Africa as well as Russia and even Pakistan and India, where the Shiite–Sunni rifts and also rifts within the Sunni world are more active than ever before.

In this situation, Prime Minister Cameron proved to be less stupid than many believe him to be: he confirmed his will to be powerful by strongly and vociferously supporting Obama and his desire to take action. Then inexplicably, especially for those who are familiar with the power of the whips in Westminster—the MPs responsible for seeing through party business in the House of Commons—he lost the Parliamentary motion by a handful of votes. The honour of the flag was intact, and intervention alongside the USA was avoided. The military misgivings were declared sacrosanct and the madness was merely put down to the many Macbeths in power throughout the world: incapable and cowardly politicians, an unclean caste to be held up for mockery by patriots. All in all, a fine piece of work.

The summer could not have ended in a worse manner, and with a game of smoke and mirrors at international level. Stooping to these games of illusion reminds me of what Britain did in the face of Chamberlain's cowardice and the Nazi-sympathising views of a king who was removed from the scene when he abdicated as a result of a fabricated marriage. But even we Italians can play the game of smoke and mirrors. It is no mere chance that the meltdown is advancing apace even in Italy. The magistrature, an order that has taken over power, shows that it is unable to govern the country as it would like: it is only able to impose vetoes, triggering fear and cowardice, but it cannot give rise to a new stable political and institutional balance, given the situation.

The situation in question is the one created by Silvio Berlusconi[2] and the judicial hounding directed against him that has now reached improbable levels. The latest demiurge to govern poor old Italy, Giorgio Napolitano,[3] is well aware of this. Everything he has done recently has been aimed at containing this order that has become a power in its own right and is also backed by powerful international supporters. As far as these supporters are concerned, however, it seems that the USA, which remains Italy's last chance of stability, has really abandoned us this time. Apart from anything else, they are in a mess similar to the one they found themselves in 1974. In my book "Southern Europe since 1945, Portugal, Spain, Italy, Greece and Turkey" (which the German Historical Institute of Rome did me the honour of commemorating, 20 years after its publication), I explained that the Portuguese military coup, which became known as the Carnation Revolution, came about in the nation where the United States had its Azores base because at

---

[2]Silvio Berlusconi, Italian ex prime Minister, has been involved in a number of legal battles. In particular, he has been (i) convicted of paying for sex with an underage prostitute and of abuse of power for asking police to release her when she was arrested for theft, and subsequently cleared of all charges; (ii) convicted of tax fraud in case focusing on the purchase of the TV rights to US films by his company, Mediaset; and (iii) acquitted in several other cases; also convicted in several, only to be cleared on appeal; others expired under statute of limitations.

[3]Giorgio Napolitano is the current President of the Italian Republic. He was elected for the first time in May 2006 and re-elected in April 2013.

that time the USA were fleeing Saigon and they were afflicted by a terrible international decadence similar to the one we are experiencing today.

Italy is much more isolated than I would personally like to believe. The *Quirinale*[4] is therefore an ivory tower, where a great political leader of the Italian Communist Party, as Giorgio Napolitano was, can only exercise his ability for long-term manoeuvres. Let me explain. Cameron lost a vote in parliament because this was the only way of not leaving the USA isolated yet abandoning them militarily. Now, in September 2013 Napolitano confounded all the admirers of his balance by appointing four life senators[5] who are looked on benevolently but can in no way be said to be politically independent. Quite the opposite: all these senators have joined their voices against those of Berlusconi and Cardinal Ruini.[6] One false step by an extremely able diplomat? I do not think so. Rather this is a gambit similar to that of Cameron. To put it bluntly, after pleasing the left, he was then able to please the right. Who could at this point blame the latest demiurge from gazing down benevolently on the fate of Silvio Berlusconi? Smoke and mirrors in a disintegrating Italy that are reflected in a disintegrating world.

---

[4]The *Quirinale*, a historic building in Rome, is the current official residence of the President of the Italian Republic. It is located on the Quirinal Hill, the highest of the seven hills of Rome.

[5]On 30 August 2013, the President of the Italian Republic Giorgio Napolitano nominated four new life senators. The Italian Senate is made of about 95 % popularly elected senators on a five-year mandate, and a remaining minority of life appointed peers. The four latest life senators are architect Renzo Piano, Nobel laureate particle physicist Carlo Rubbia, world-renowned music conductor Claudio Abbado and pharmacology professor and stem-cell research expert Elena Cattaneo. These four personalities would, according to Napolitano, act in "absolute independence" and bring their contributions to highly significant areas in institutional life. Berlusconi's party The People of Freedom harshly criticised the appointment of these four senators. One of the reasons was that all four new senators had been critical towards Berlusconi in the past, even though they never openly aligned themselves with the centre-left. If the four of them had voted in favour of the Democratic Party in the Senate, this would have changed the numbers in the upper chamber in quite a significant way: now the leftist Democratic Party needed merely 7 votes in order to have a majority that did not include Berlusconi's party. 7 votes were likely to be obtained from 7 "dissidents" from Beppe Grillo's 5 Star Movement, willing to vote with the Democratic Party.

[6]Camillo Ruini is an Italian cardinal of the Catholic Church. On 14 February 2006, he was confirmed as president of the Italian Episcopal Conference by Pope Benedict XVI a post at which he served until March 2007.

The publication of a book by Timothy Geithner "Stress test. Reflections in Financial Crisis" (Random House Business Books, London 2014) has now become clear evidence of the depths reached, not only by the opinion of a public that knows little about the politics it observes only through a keyhole or through the rose-tinted lenses of the ideological furore that could be applied to more noble causes, always allowing for the fact that a furore indicates any real virtue. Everyone was astounded by the publication of the famous phrase or rather the small section of the book recounting exactly what happened a few months before the resignation of Silvio Berlusconi's government, which brought into being the period that I referred to as the Roman dictatorship, after the Roman senatorial dictatorships of bygone times, when the choice fell upon Mario Monti[7]—who went on to offer innumerable examples of his unparalleled human and civic worth to the Italian people and everyone who appointed him—through a process of coopting that was as extraordinary as it was unusual. The economic truth surfaced. The conflict was intra-European, between Germany and France and the Scandinavian countries on the one hand and Italy governed by Silvio Berlusconi and Giulio Tremonti[8] on the other. The dominant nations had no desire to help Italy to overcome a crisis that was much less severe than the Teutonic deflationist liberal order believed (Italy was a patient with a mild fever), but did wish to save the French and German banks, which were patients with a dangerously high fever, due to their commitments to Greece, which was hanging perilously close to the brink of an imposed default.

I have said more than once that the international financial oligarchy and its direct political representatives, in other words the cusps of German and French power ably supported by German deflation and the Bundesbank, saw the true enemy not as Berlusconi but as Tremonti. He persisted with a struggle against the German deflationary superpower that may have been solitary and dissimulating,

---

[7]President Giorgio Napolitano appointed Professor Mario Monti life senator on 9 November 2011. On 12 November 2011, following Berlusconi's resignation, Napolitano asked Monti to form a new government. Monti accepted and held talks with the leaders of the main Italian political parties, declaring that he wanted to form a government that would remain in office until the next scheduled general elections in 2013. On 16 November 2011, Monti was sworn in as Prime Minister of Italy, with a technocratic cabinet composed entirely of unelected professionals.

[8]Giulio Tremonti served in the government of Italy as Minister of Economy and Finances under Prime Minister Silvio Berlusconi from 1994 to 1995, from 2001 to 2004, from 2005 to 2006, and from 2008 to 2011.

but was no less dangerous for this: he predicted a meltdown and denounced the inefficacy of the ECB's restrictive policies.

All these things may be clearly read in the documents set out in the appendices to his penultimate book "Exit Strategy". Of course, we are entitled to wonder who benefits, who benefited, from Geithner's statements, but it is clear. It is clear not if we think of Italian policy but of the Libyan tragedy where an attempt is being made to reconstruct a military backbone against the fanatical, murderous Muslim superpower. It is clear if we think of Nigeria, where fundamentalist forces move directly to perform actions of symbolic challenge to the West; Algeria, immovable and safe but sitting on a social volcano; and the Crimea, which risks escalating a failure to reach a diplomatic agreement after the collapse of the USSR into a radical crisis that could overturn all of Europe.

But Europe continues to play the violin as the Titanic sinks and reveals a lack of any strategic will to face up to the dangers that emerge from these crises. We need only consider that Italy risks permanent decline due to closure of the Suez Canal and that we Italians do not even have any naval potential to speak of at all, a potential that would do us a lot more good than any F35: if our ships cannot pass through the Suez Canal, we can wave goodbye to Italy! The USA must conclude an imperial design with two horns: an Atlantic horn embodied by the understanding between the USA and Europe, to counterbalance the other very difficult horn that must take shape in the Pacific to contain an increasingly aggressive China. This is the reason why books like Geithner's are being published: to give Italian politicians a short, sharp shock so that they realise the threat they pose to the entire Western world, with the USA at its head—with their blandness, their indecisiveness and their failure to give successive governments democratic legitimacy.

The USA could not withstand a Mediterranean crisis with the waves of migrants and political refugees who are already pouring into Italy and from there into Europe. One way that the USA is conducting an indirect battle against the deflationary Merkel is by intervening directly in Italian politics. And they believe that the stakes are so high that Grillo's party[9] is worthy of support for setting the

---

[9] Giuseppe Piero "Beppe" Grillo is an Italian comedian, actor, blogger and political activist. He has been involved in political activity since 2009 as founder of the Italian political Five Star Movement, in order to bring together, via the Internet, people who share his ideals about honesty and direct democracy, and saying that politicians are the servants of the people and that they should work for the country only for a short time, that they should not have criminal records and that they should focus their attention on the problems of the country without any conflict of interest.

entire system of Italian power and subsequently European power into motion once again. If the "Berlusconi-Tremonti" scandal can be used for this purpose, then we have nothing to lose.

This gambit is certainly not without risk, but possibly less risky than one would believe. I am old enough to remember the days when we had to sleep away from home in a different bed every night due to the threat of the Red Brigades[10] and the assassinations that took place in my own city of Turin, with the infamous masters who now feature in the headlines and hold positions of power. All Grillo is doing is telling his followers to become elected within democratic institutions and behind his colourful language I fail to see guns or cold-blooded murderers but often a lot of well-meaning, civic-minded people who want to improve things for themselves and make the world a better place. Yet again the USA is giving a hand to a country that is struggling to become a nation, in this case Italy, which is struggling to rediscover its spirit because it has lost its soul…It is nevertheless worth saying at this point that Italy is revealing an unexpected gift for political revival.

Many people are wondering what is happening in Italy after a special Senate committee met on 4 October to vote that Silvio Berlusconi should be declared unfit for public office after his sentence and excluded from politics. At the same time, the Letta-Alfano[11] government did not lose a vote of confidence by Berlusconi's followers but was voted in by them: the majority of them showing a political desire to separate their fate from that of the demiurge and the tycoon, the minority using last minute tactics. Parliamentarians from a large personality-led party resigned as a protest against a sentence that had obviously been coming for years and could not in any way have been avoided. Machiavelli[12] said that you

---

[10]Red Brigades, Italian Brigate Rosse, militant left-wing organization in Italy that gained notoriety in the 1970s for kidnappings, murders and sabotage. Its self-proclaimed aim was to undermine the Italian state and pave the way for a Marxist upheaval led by a "revolutionary proletariat". In 1978, the Red Brigades kidnapped and killed the leader of the Christian Democratic Party, Aldo Moro.

[11]On 24 April 2013, Italian President of the Republic, Giorgio Napolitano, gave to the vice-secretary of the Democratic Party, Enrico Letta, the task of forming a government, having determined that Pier Luigi Bersani, leader of the winning coalition, could not form a government because it did not have a majority in the Senate. Angelino Alfano was Vice Prime Minister.

[12]Niccolò di Bernardo dei Machiavelli (1469–1527) was an Italian historian, politician, diplomat, philosopher, humanist and writer based in Florence during the Renaissance. Although it is relatively short, the treatise is the most remembered of Machiavelli's works and the one most responsible for bringing the word "Machiavellian" into usage as a pejorative. "Machiavellianism" is a widely used negative term to characterise unscrupulous politicians of the sort Machiavelli described in *The Prince*.

should not leave your enemies wounded but kill them, otherwise their bitterness will cause them to become more destructive than ever. The prophecy turned out to be true. Despite all the calls and appeals for caution, the chickens came home to roost. The paradigmatic power shift towards a judiciary that is now a power in its own right and no longer an order has been fully exposed as a destructive factor. Of course, Berlusconi should take a step back. Everyone says so, but no one finds themselves in his situation, which is paradigmatic of the slow and inexorable destruction of the symmetry of powers in a modern state and the breakdown of the relationship between justice and politics and the power of politics and within politics.

The government is faltering and no longer seeks to appease. It divides and swings. The President of the Republic is a Shakespearean character: Macbeth and Lear are both evident by turns in the torment, which remains unique and cannot be put into words, as illustrated by the silence observed by Giorgio Napolitano during the celebrations for Bettino Craxi,[13] which by no coincidence was held during the same period. The very occasion was poignant, with looming clouds and memories and heavy, leaden skies, symbolic of the fate of a state that is no longer able to find itself.

Meanwhile, the Democratic Party is unable to find itself either: it is also swinging between personality-led parties and left-over groupings of former *Dorotei*[14] and *Forze Nuove*[15] factions… in a manner of speaking… intended naturally, as a metaphor and without any claim to historical accuracy. This means that two very important historical opportunities are being wasted: the first, the end of political unity between Catholics, who have changed from being a bright sun into a sticky web of power and the second, the end of the Soviet communist culture, which has changed from being about revolutionary or reformist socialism to a

---

[13]Bettino Craxi, byname of Benedetto Crax (1934–2000), Italian politician who became his nation's first Socialist prime minister (1983–1987). In February 1993, multiple charges of political corruption forced Craxi to resign his post as party leader. He never denied that he had illegally solicited money for the Socialist Party but claimed that all the political parties had done so and that the Socialists were being targeted for political reasons. Craxi left Italy for Tunisia later that year, just before being convicted for some of the charges. He never returned to Italy.

[14]Dorotei, were a leading faction of the Italian Christian Democrat party (DC) which took its name from the convent of Saint Dorotea in which it was founded in 1959.

[15]Forze Nuove, leftist faction of the Italian Christian Democrat party (DC) led by Mr. Carlo Donat Cattin.

form of compromise that overlooks everything in a purely personal power struggle. The few believers have become dispersed and lack a church. If they ever want to find one they must first of all find themselves. In the meantime, however, the international division of labour marches on: it is implacable with its international historical organisations to continue the Italian campaign.

We can learn from Machiavelli here too: the French were called in to fight Venice and became a fearsome obstacle that was only warded off by the astuteness and greatness of a mighty Pope. Now we are missing that astuteness and that greatness—but not the little popes, unfortunately—and so the French et al. continue to bivouac at the last campfires, which are still smoking despite the rain of judicial terror on the landlines or mobile phones that carry not only data and voice signals but that also hold together the security and legal unity of a nation: they howl into the wind because they are uprooted. The banks controlled by the foundations, in other words by the new invisible and personal politics of the fraternities, have suddenly decided to scurry back to their accounting! Just as the armies appear on the battlefield: the banks and financial institutions withdraw to leave room for the new occupants. It is another form of resignation. *Anabasis*[16] should be required reading in an Italy that is withdrawing and losing its own identity.

From the USA to Italy, schism perennially lays the grounds for dissolution, which is extremely hard to escape, however hard we try.

The difficulties are not only internal to Italy's culture and history but also emerge forcefully from the European context within which Italy—a nation that is essential to the Mediterranean civilisation and therefore a strategic linchpin of the Western world—is forced into reckless and hasty technocratic and monetary unification with disastrous consequences.

The depth of the economic meltdown that has been brewing for centuries and now has Europe in its grip reveals certain opportunities with the power to overcome not so much the crisis but rather the institutional and political conditions aggravated by the crisis. The consequences of this are extremely grim, not only

---

[16]Xenophon, the Athenian, was born in 431 B.C. He was a pupil of Socrates. He marched with the Spartans and was exiled from Athens. Sparta gave him land and property in Scillus, where he lived for many years before having to move once more, to settle in Corinth. He died in 354 B.C. The Anabasis is his story of the March to Persia to aid Cyrus, who enlisted Greek help to try and take the throne from Artaxerxes, and the ensuing return of the Greeks, in which Xenophon played a leading role. This occurred between 401 B.C. and March 399 B.C.

within Europe but throughout the world, first and foremost with regard to the USA and its inevitable role. The European elections of May 2014 were an event that will have radical consequences in the future although they will not, of course, have any repercussions—apart from extremely cautious and moderate ones—on the depth of the economic and moral crisis afflicting Europe. It is certainly true that the European People's Party will undoubtedly lose a good number of seats, but under the guidance of its Austro-German and Scandinavian membership, it is arguably the culture that bears the heaviest responsibility for the ECB's deflationary policy, for excessively nationalist politics and for creating a common vision of Europe as a withdrawal of sovereignty instead of a sharing of sovereignty, as we have recently seen in Greece and every day in the policies of the commissioners; if all this is indeed true, the European People's Party did not lose out at the ballot box. All the analysts are tearing their hair out due to the success of the Eurosceptics. But the real issues are different and much more complicated than they appear at first sight. One thing needs to be said at the outset: the PES missed the chance of signing up for a form of Euroscepticism that strongly believes that the destiny of Europe should be firmly anchored to continental Keynesian policy, a Euroscepticism based on the reform of the ECB and on absolute power ultimately conferred on Parliament and not on the committees. This Euroscepticism would have had its own dignity and would have clipped the wings of the right-wing neo-Bonapartists who have sprouted like so many harmless mushrooms and poisonous toadstools. It is no coincidence that the PES was also shunned by the electorate and more heavily than the EPP.

Now we will review the anti-European movements in order. Firstly, we will take a look outside the Euro zone, in other words at the UK where sterling rules instead of the euro and common law prevails. Labour is the leading party and when we think back to the pro-Blair litanies, proclaiming him as the saviour, it is a good sign that Ed Miliband is not Blairite and has brought together the party and the trade unions, rebuilding a strong reformist force that could be a good model for the Italian Democratic Party (PD), for example. The Tories are the second party. They could have stolen many votes from Farrage's anti-European UKIP party were it not for the fact that Cameron is such a dull leader. In the UK, the big news is the collapse of the Liberals, which in any case has been expected for some time.

Now for France. Here, the most important factor is of course the extraordinary rise of Marine Le Pen. If you read her programme with care, if you examine the profiles of her candidates, as the French press have done, you will see that Marine has continued along the same trajectory that she embarked upon at the recent French administrative elections: strong national values both in terms of economic policy and immigration, no more anti-Semitism and racism. Paradoxically, these are the same new values espoused by President Hollande, when he recently confirmed the appointment of Arnaud Mountebourg as Minister of the Economy calling for a return to the *Régie Nationale*, and the recent appointment of Manuel Valls as the new Prime Minister, with his tough stance on immigrants and criminals. The electorate naturally preferred Le Penn to Valls, particularly on matters of security and immigration. The collapse of the post-Gaullists was unexpected. Everything will be up for grabs again, though, at the coming political elections with the two-round system, which will bring new hope to the Socialists, the neo-Gaullists and maybe even the neo-centrists. In any case, Le Pen's victory is the most significant event. This can be explained by the wide-ranging, strong and solid roots that the French right-wing has been able to bring to bear at crucial moments of French history, unlike the socialist and subsequently the communist tradition. The problem today in France is that only the right-wing is making culture and this, as not many people seem to realise, is important because there has always been a relationship between high and low culture and people, the common people have always been influenced by this relationship. Unimaginative TV commentators use Le Pen's triumph as an excuse for claiming that the French–German axis no longer exists. In actual fact, another French–German axis, which is much more important for the fate of the world, is forming down on the banks of the upper Niger River in the heart of black Africa, where France and Germany continue with implacable conviction to fight off the Chinese presence.

Spain notched up only one win for its "indignant" movement, with the downscaling of the people's and socialist parties. In Catalonia, I would point to the victory of the left-over *Convergencia y Union*, a nationalist centre-right party, which suggests an independentist approach very different from the one originally predicted.

In the rest of Europe, right-wing parties did very well in Holland, Austria and Hungary, in the latter case with a self-avowedly anti-Semitic and Nazi party. The same thing happened in the Scandinavian countries. Those who are aware of the history of the European right-wing were not surprised by this, because they are aware that in countries where there is no history of a strong and well-established socialist and communist left-wing, the right-wing has always roamed the range, giving those who believe in the individual and in liberty sleepless nights. Importantly, the only country where this did not happen is Sweden, where the social democrats returned to power with a socialist programme that can only be described as old school, in other words based on a welfare state, deficit spending, neo-communitarian but also neo-statist, anti-deflationist and antiliberal, which only goes to show that when socialism goes back to representing the common people, it not only wins but also means that the common people do not show their worst side, exemplified by the neo-Nazis and neo-fascists, but their best side, as is embodied by popular Christian and socialist values.

The real new Europe is, however, emerging in its cultural birthplace, Greece. Here, Syriza has become the leading party with the centre-right in second place, the Socialists in third place and, bringing up the rear with 9 % of the vote, Golden Dawn, in other words a party like the neo-Nazi, anti-Semitic Hungarian party. Here in Greece, poor Papandreou was forced to resign a couple of years ago when, as a socialist prime minister, he announced that he wished to hold a referendum on the measures introduced by the Troika and since then has disappeared without trace—the PASOK was destroyed at the time when Berlusconi and Tremonti were forced out of office, with Merkel wailing, Obama acting like a boss, but unable to achieve anything, stating, "We cannot have his blood on our hands", as Geithner revealed in his book of memoirs. Despite this, nobody got the blood of the Greek politicians on their hands and the people were able to vote. This now means that the only real rational alternative to the European People's Party and its disastrous economic and political strategies has won a resounding victory and is the leading party. It is entirely another matter in Italy. In my opinion, the crux of the Italian European political elections was the coming together of the following strands. The first strand was the fact that the people were able to go back to the ballot boxes after the *coup d'état* against Berlusconi and Tremonti led Thai style by the President of the Republic with the artificial, Faustian creation of the little man Monti, fortunately without the army being involved. And look what the result was: Matteo Renzi,[17] "a fast-talking performer", as he was described by the Financial Times, was then able to take 40 % of the vote, in other words Bersani's 30 % plus Monti's 10 %, as happened in the political elections of February 2013: elections that not even a King of Thailand could have opposed. But let us examine the second strand, which is that Renzi's PD, with its 40 % of the vote, beats all records: it is the leading European political party; it is the leading European Socialist party and can therefore lay claim to a high number of seats in the European Parliament, which will really allow it to stand in the way of the PPE's policies; it is the only party able to stand up to Merkel and gather around itself a true Keynesian and anti-Blairite socialist alternative in order to rebuild a new Europe. The problem we face is whether Matteo Renzi and his companions will really be able to achieve all this, in other words free themselves of the neo-liberal, financial

---

[17]Matteo Renzi, present leader of the Democratic Party and Prime Minister of the Italian Government since 22 February 2014.

order and neo-Bonapartist dross that are appearing in the ranks of their middle managers and leaders. One thing is without doubt, however, Renzi marks a victory for Italian Democratic Catholicism. On many fronts, as I have emphasised on other occasions, it is emblematic that a Catholic took the PD into the PES, and this is a mark of infinite freedom for which all Italians should be grateful: the party unity of the Catholics is dead and buried at last. The second victory is again that of democratic Catholicism over what remained of the glorious Catholic communist tradition, in other words nothing is left of it. This very transformation saw the political disappearance of Mario Monti and his incredible followers and delivered an extremely hard blow to *Forza Italia* and Berlusconi. The consequence was that this unprecedented victory by democratic Catholicism cut the claws of Beppe Grillo and his nice boys and girls, who are divided between rabble-rousers and men and women of good faith. Let us keep a sense of perspective, however, Grillo has definitely changed from a movement to a party and this means that the moment of truth has also arrived for his Five Star Movement. Will it remain a Bonapartist protest party or will it become a left-wing party, to the left of the PD? This would be a shocking twist for those who have always believed that Italy is by nature a moderate country. But in the words of a great Pope[18]: "we must not be afraid". We must indeed never forget that Matteo Renzi's extraordinary victory is first and foremost a European victory. Not merely because the elections were European but because fidelity to Europe was the message that the Italian Prime Minister wished to give to his country and because the working policies reported to the government staff and the media at the very outset were European.

Continuing in order, the PD is the strongest party in Europe with 40.8 % of the vote, followed by the German CDU with 35.3 %. Lagging behind this leading pair come the Spanish and Danish People's Parties with 26 %. The fundamental matter that we cannot overlook is that a European Socialist party is being led by a young Catholic who has put paid to the myth of party unity amongst Catholics and has, following in the footsteps of Jacques Delors, breathed new life into a virtuous tradition that we hope is not destined to remain a minority. In any case, the development will bear fruit because it will make it possible to operate not only in opposition to the CDU and other people's parties but also through asymmetrical cooperation with the same parties over certain crucial matters that are bound to crop up as the crisis progresses. On the other hand, Marine Le Pen's nationalist triumph in France with 25 % of the vote undoubtedly downgraded

---

[18]Pope John Paul II was Pope of the Catholic Church from 16 October 1978 until his death on 2 April 2005.

the French–German axis with the disastrous defeat of Hollande's Socialists, who only achieved 14 %. There is therefore room to pursue a new policy together with Spain, where the Socialists achieved 26 %, and Greece, where Syriza leapt into first place with 26.6 % and policies that are much more reasonable and sensible than an overhasty press would have us believe.

Ultimately we will no longer operate in accordance with national blocks, or rather, we should no longer reason in terms of national blocks but in terms of alliances whose geometry is determined by problems as they arise, based on socialist or people's political families instead of on nationalist discriminating factors.

This would still make it possible to represent national interests, but with more room for manoeuvre and a form of bargaining that is not a win–lose game but one involving a system of weights and counterweights and interest compensation. I will give an example. We will certainly be able to find agreement between socialist parties, including Syriza, over the revolutionary Keynesian policy of macro-investment in public works that Matteo Renzi immediately and boldly announced that he will present in Europe during Italy's six month EU presidency, but it may also be supported by more than a few European people's parties, not merely the Spanish, for example, but possibly even the Germans and Austrians. The Germans will be conditioned not only by their own culture but also by the alliance in progress within Germany with the SPD, which cannot be ignored in Europe. It will be more difficult to achieve a virtuous crosscutting effect over the inevitable reform of the ECB, where nationalist claims may prevail amongst the Germans and Scandinavians, and where the hope of turning Mario Draghi from a diligent spokesperson with magical qualities into a genuine Federal Reserve style central banker will require much tougher battles and the rediscovery of the great force represented by ideology in politics, which has been forgotten and overlooked for too long.

To sum up, we will return to making great politics and this is the greatest virtue of Renzi's victory. When he says that he wishes to restore Italy's dignity within Europe, we are bound to back him because it is in Europe itself that we must overcome the clichéd thinking that made the Italians inept and cowardly, when they fell for the infamous theory that the Italians had to be saved from themselves through an external shock in the form of Europe. This victory by Renzi may really see the start of a new Europe, beginning with Italy strengthening the admirable qualities that Italians can still be proud of in the men and women in power and thus damping down the rebelliousness and subversiveness of Grillo and his companions. Who knows, his movement could even change into a force that is gradually able to make the most of his best fresh and clean young energies, overcoming its obscure Bonapartist and Caesarean origins. As we are reminded by great European constitutionalists such as Benjamin Constant, the greatest of them all, institutions are set up to create in men those virtues that they are unable to express by themselves: whilst moderating their defects, they emphasise their attributes and transform them. This is what we need, as Italians and as Europeans: to become institutionalised. We can do this in the first place by changing the European institutions in accordance with the beliefs of Constant: full powers of enforcement to Parliament and only the power of guarantee to the committees; a return to the healthy concept of a mixed economy, overcoming the liberalist order that led to pro-cyclicality in the crisis with overwhelming unemployment; foregrounding in Europe and in Italy of the duties—above all—as well as the rights of citizens. This is the deep European significance of the victory scored by Matteo Renzi's Democratic Party. It has been a victory for great catholic and socialist reformist ideas that can now achieve fusion only if they can be deployed from a continental perspective, thus helping to restore to Europe what it deserves, in other words an international role in the alliance with the USA.

Start of the Mediterranean Crisis

Yet the plight of the Mediterranean area remains extremely serious. Everything began with events that appeared—to most people—to be auspicious for reconstruction.

The wave of collective mobilisation that struck North Africa is like a huge flock of birds blotting out the sky. From afar, their solid mass is strikingly oppressive: they look like the grey sky in a Permeke painting. But as soon as we see the flock from closer up, our perspective changes.

The solid mass resolves to reveal the scales of a complex and continually asymmetrical fractal. Let me explain: this has come about because North Africa is one of the most diversified human ecosystems in the world with very clear fault lines if we immediately examine matters from a state perspective. This is the case in most of the areas affected by revolts, albeit with unequal intensity and multifaceted institutional configurations. Events in Egypt and Tunisia have nevertheless shown us that the state is what it is and its existence does not depend on the physical person holding power. Its physical or symbolic disappearance (ousting from power) does not culminate in the death of the institution, which goes on to replicate itself. This is essential for the continuity of business. In all cases, the army guarantees this continuity, constituting the very backbone of the state, but with two variants. The armies in this post-colonial and post-Arabian culture fall into one of the following two moulds: revolutionary (Algeria and Egypt) or monarchical-sacred (the Royal family in Morocco and in Jordan are hereditary lineages that claim their descendancy from the Prophet and the army's loyalty is thus twofold: to the monarch and to the Prophet). Both the armies, Algerian and

Egyptian, are of revolutionary origin, but now they have little national independence and are highly dependent on the West (primarily the USA and France). The greater the Western influence on the army, the more state continuity means business continuity: we have learnt this from Egypt. The moral of this story is that any transition to democracy (?) and any continuity in economic relations is bound to come to grips with the army, in other words the relationship between the business community and the army must be considered.

Another important issue is the clear inability of these countries to achieve economic development and therefore growth that is even only moderately unequal and only moderately imbalanced, despite their great national resources: mainly fossil hydrocarbons and certain mineral resources (Moroccan phosphates, for example). One contributing cause is not the economy but social stratification and the outcome of the post-colonial political struggle. This has given rise to a *rentier* and bourgeois class who act as brokers between national resources and their international exploitation, hence the family and clan trappings that parasitically cling to the state armies and bureaucracy. Egypt is a textbook example of this situation, with its sprawling state–family–patronage-based bureaucracy.

Lastly, we are left with the most explosive problem, which is the fuse that has been lit in Tunisia and lies at the basis of the revolt: the formation throughout North Africa of an intellectual sub-proletariat that has led to a genuinely new inter-class aspect of the revolt and is at the same time the untapped resource of the area: knowledge combined with youth may give rise to a passion for development if it is given an outlet in the dignity of employment. The danger is that this may occur with devastating consequences for the instability of those societies. Employment must be the first commitment for those acting in these countries; otherwise, all their plans are doomed to failure. We are then left with Libya, which is a case in its own right: tribalism, archaic social relationships, absence of the state of western origin and the personalistic continuity of a power that has changed from revolutionary to a presence so brooding that it is at the point of swallowing up the tribal children of the revolution. The first task should be to prevent the "Somalisation" of Libya and seek to fully understand the specific features of the case and in other words to change from economy to anthropology.

World Economic Crisis

The living anthropology of the Mediterranean crisis is written into the world economic crisis. But the world economy is hovering on the brink of madness. The financial crisis is nothing more than a snowball that causes an avalanche to thunder down on the houses of the national states huddled in the valley bottom. Even the USA, despite dominating the valley, is subject to unprecedented internal tensions over public debt. For anyone who thinks with their head, the spectacle of the proposals implemented or announced to cope with what amounts to a radical restructuring of world capitalism based on very high-risk financial dominion is devastating. Faced with this restructuring, the thousands of highly paid economists beavering away in international institutions are unable to do anything but trot out recipes that we all know off by heart by now: liberalise and privatise, especially the labour market; cut political costs (listen to who's talking about costs!); cut public spending; set no limits to the transferability of capital; do not attack the incestuous structure of the great world banks that apply excessive leverage using the money of their account holders, continually causing the slaughter of innocents, but instead regulate them from the top-down in a new version of the ineffectual GOSPLAN. It is unclear whether they are crafty or just plain stupid: none of these remedies have had any impact at all on the growth that we need to restructure public debt.

This doubt becomes even more pertinent when we hear about ideas such as that of prohibiting short selling, when everyone knows that most immediate share transfer deals take place in millionths of a second through "dark pools", in other words the unregulated electronic circuits that business banks update through ultra-fine tuning. This plethora of "experts" is divided into two great cohorts.

Those who orchestrated the German takeover of Europe through the raising of rates and the out-and-out mad people who say that the danger lies not in international deflation but in inflation, whilst the Greek chorus of the ECB fans the flames of the crisis instead of putting them out.

Followers of the FED have another plan in mind: to support growth by inflating debt to the point that it is possible to exploit beyond all reason the true competitive edge of the USA: their world power (in this the Republicans are stupid to force a default even if they do free themselves of Obama). Through this world power they will then be able to disseminate growth internationally by expanding liquidity and ensuring a gradual return to the only thing that can save us: inflation (Bernanke's targeting of inflation).

Greenspan's memoir makes inspiring reading in this regard and reveals that continued dominion of the West as well as North American growth is central to his thinking. This continuity should be our common goal, but it can be achieved only by laying the grounds for new growth at world level and therefore also in Europe and Italy. World trade figures are not encouraging in this respect: absolute levels are slowly declining and the BRICS countries are no longer the driving force they once were.

A fast and drastic reduction of tax on employment and capital is therefore an indispensable counterpart to the increase in the taxation on luxury goods instead of on people. Only in this way will growth be possible, and we will be able to slowly turn the world cycle towards manufacturing instead of towards finance. Short-term speculative investments must be taxed transparently and immediately. With regard to debt in the strict sense of the word, the welfare reform must be based on raising the age at which both men and women leave work to after 65 years of age as well as relaunching mutualism and family saving.

And now we come to the crux of the matter that divides all of us. I believe that the euro should be subject to a serious appraisal with regard to its sustainability within Europe as a whole and also within the countries that have always been outside its French and German heartland: in other words southern Europe and all of Italy. This is an inevitable examination of conscience now that a period of very slow growth or a decline in growth is opening up before us. A stateless single currency may lead the patient towards his final death-throes and not towards recovery.

The Chickens Have Come Home to Roost

Many chickens have come home to roost throughout the world, in a day of reckoning that began on an international scale and ended up as national crisis, confirming the accuracy of theories that suggest the bond between nation and internationalisation is crucial to understanding the guiding themes of history.

Firstly, if we take a look at the world through the eyes of an economy hardwired into the loop of international politics, we can see two main effects. The first is the turn taken by globalisation. The sustained growth rate of the BRICS countries has not reached its end but the end of the first growth phase, as we learn from Kaldor's growth laws and Myrdal's theories. Rapid growth based on capital goods and the creation of urban working and middle classes is over. In non-communist countries this has brought into being a peasant and agricultural bourgeois class that makes it possible to pass from growth based on the accumulation of capital goods to growth based also on consumption arising as a result of the agricultural reforms typical of nations such as Brazil and India, albeit to a lesser extent and much less organised in terms of private ownership. This is particularly true of India, which is still dominated by a very strong community culture.

Indian backwardness in relation to the internal market and in the field of monetary circulation has recently exploded and taken by surprise all who those who believe that it is possible to understand economy by reading statistics and not by studying history and anthropology. Most Indians do not trade money but goods and even money is not normally hoarded in banks. The recent victory by Narendra Modi, leader of the Bharatiya Janata Party—the Hindu Nationalist Party—on a ticket of liberalisation, opening up of the internal market and new foreign investments, coupled with the collapse of the historical Congress Party dominated for decades by the Gandhi family, is a particularly significant event because it assumes important strategic relevance: will something similar happen in Brazil and South Africa? For now, the economic transformation has only had radical political consequences in India. In South Africa, the party that is heir to Mandela held firmly onto power in the latest elections and it is difficult to imagine that the tables will be turned in the great South American power, even after the relative decline of the PT, the dominant party, due to the urban middle-class uprisings. The new approach that Modi immediately imposed on Indian foreign policy came as a surprise though, with initiatives designed to encourage good neighbourliness, in other words a reduction in the decades-old tensions between India and Pakistan, which is a nerve centre for the control of military operations in Central Asia, and Bengal. These movements were undoubtedly aimed at reducing the recent rapprochement with the USA as a bulwark against the Chinese and Russians that had been so typical of recent Indian foreign policy. It is difficult to say whether the Hindu nationalist electoral victory will mark a true step forward by India.

The growing level of interrelationship in the world economy reveals all the limitations of backwardness in the field of monetary circulation. The very fact of growth itself highlights the problem and this situation brings about the depreciation of a currency that is hardly ever hoarded. Those of us who do not believe that everything is always in balance, from the USA, to India and Papua New Guinea, were expecting it...

China, on the other hand, has ended up in a real dead-end because no agricultural bourgeoisie has grown up and her cities are filling with illegal non-citizens who cannot consume as the urban masses should. This means that China is falling into all the traps of countries that have bureaucratic economies and state capitalism and are led by terrorist dictatorships: initial decadence due to production overcapacity of capital goods magnified by the disastrous revolution in finance, which destabilised an age-old balance whilst creating world asymmetries when the Middle Kingdom joined the WTO in 2001. This led to the collapse of the unequal post-Bretton Woods ratio between world metropolitan economies and peripheral world economies. The asymmetrical competition has now become an obstacle to the growth of China itself, which is unable to create an internal market, whilst—paradoxically—it is exporting forced labour throughout the world in a quest for the energy and cultivable land that it is unable to produce at home due to its own bureaucratic/terrorist-led economy.

The chaos afflicting Russia is different: this country is suffering from the isolation of a great and solitary prisoner nation stuck between a hostile Europe that wants its energy resources but prevents it from expanding as a result of crazy rules against competition (all of European industry being in decline due to falling margins and failure to consolidate due to fear of being accused of the sin of monopoly, having forgotten Sylos Labini's holy text on oligopoly and technical progress...) and China, with which it is forced to bargain due to refusal by the USA and Europe to reshape the face of the world in the wake of the Cold War. They in fact believed that it was possible to continue to produce growth whilst excluding Russia from Europe and the world market: Russia was not admitted to the WTO until 2011, ratifying the USA's tragic inability to understand the new world order after Reagan and Gorbachev. In this way, by not pursuing the Gaullist aim of a Europe stretching from the Atlantic to the Urals—a device for preventing European decadence—this great Eurasian nation was forced into a disastrous embrace with China.

But we need to think more about the matter. The origins of the Russian–Chinese rapprochement lie completely in European policy, as is demonstrated by the Ukraine crisis and Russia's de facto occupation of the Crimea through a form of hybrid warfare; in other words, one based on the establishment and defence of a Russian community in the Ukraine, which is in turn devastated by the street battle triggered by the argument over whether a gigantic country with deep Russian Orthodox roots and divided into age-old national factions, as we saw in World War II, should or should not join the European Union. In any case the German–Russian energy and manufacturing *Kombinat* fortuitously exercises on Putin and Lavrov, the great Russian foreign minister, a pressure that is much greater than that of any European diplomacy and acts alongside the weight of EU diplomacy. The incredible Baroness Ashton, Foreign Minister of Kakania,[1] could have prevented the annexing of the Crimea and the struggles in the Ukraine by simply taking action at the first inkling of crisis to assure Putin and his economic and military power bloc that the EU would commit itself to preserving the use of the Sebastopol base in the Crimea for the Russians irrespective of the political situation in the Ukraine. Russia has in any case hung onto the base by paying a colossal rent, as it does with the nuclear base in Kazakhstan. The Cold War climate that is making itself felt throughout Europe cannot fail to have extremely heavy consequences on the financial situation.

---

[1] Kakania is the ironic name writer Robert Musil gave to what was known as the Austro-Hungarian Empire of Franz Joseph. Empire of many ethnic groups, in contrast with each other, driven by a corrupt government, collapsed with the First World War. The derision, due to the image evoked by the sound of the word Kakania, is clear in all European languages.

In the face of all this, we can only be astounded by the schizophrenia of the USA. Heedless of the wise warnings by Kissinger, who was well aware of what a sophisticated intellectual like Sergei Karaganov has been saying for years about its syndrome of encircling post-Communist Russia, having forgotten the healthy realism of the Westphalian school of diplomacy, the USA is swinging from a monocratic approach to a delegatory approach. An example of the former approach is the meeting between Lavrov and Kerry that took place in Rome at the time of the talks on Libya, whilst on the same day a meeting was held in Brussels over the Ukraine affair, thus effectively sidelining the EU. This sidelining was also confirmed by the confrontational decision to send fighter aircraft to Polish bases that already have their missiles pointing towards Russia. At the same time, USA inability to translate the meetings and the threats into concrete and realistic proposals opens the way to bargaining based entirely on currency and trade goods, which is orchestrated by Mrs. Merkel whenever she puts on her broker's hat. Anyone believing that the Ukraine affair can be resolved by promising €11 billion to the new government is making a big mistake. And here we again see the USA adopting a delegatory approach, since whilst it is concerned on one hand with German-style deflationary European economic policy, it is actually delegating manoeuvres with regard to the Ukraine, with predictably disastrous results. Making Europeans in the B team tighten their belts whilst conducting diplomacy through charitable works can only enrage the common people and those sectors of the population already exasperated by the constant, tenacious and blind destruction of the European social model, pursued by Frau Merkel and her longstanding voiceless cronies.

A few months before the crisis exploded in the Ukraine and Crimea, Putin made a visit to Italy. The full implications of the possible intrinsic strategic value of this visit were not fully grasped at the time. Due to the standing of the character involved and the fact that the implications of the event were not merely economic, the picture that emerged looked rosy but extremely complicated. Russia certainly had achieved two very important positive diplomatic results. The first one was and is the agreement drawn up with Assad's Syria—and I mean Assad's Syria and not the Syria of the rebels or one of their representatives—over the elimination of chemical weapons. Although the agreement actually illustrates the decisive role played by Russia alongside the large- and medium-sized powers, the regional powers—in other words Saudi Arabia, Qatar, the United Arab Emirates, Turkey and above all Israel—viewed and continue to view this agreement in a bad light because it implicitly frees up the Shiite factions. The growth of Shiite power can now be immensely multiplied due to the new regional role that their guide state can perform. Iran is a much more evolved and developed power than any other Gulf state: Persia is Persia and only agreement between the great Arab, Turkish and Persian cultures can appease what is the most strategically important region in the world in terms of energy and in terms of the spiritual values that reside in the State of Israel and the Holy Places of Christianity and of Islam. Israel understands this better than anyone and its position, which we can decide not to share, is not farsighted, particularly in the wake of the agreement with Iran over uranium enrichment. All this was naturally done with the USA playing a key role, as was the case in Syria: North American reluctance effectively opened the way to Russian mediation. Together with Germany, France, the United Kingdom and Russia, the USA played a decisive role. Incidentally, Italy was still remarkable by its absence at that time! But now let us come to the geostrategic nub of the matter raised by Putin's visit in the light of these events: the paradox before our eyes was that whilst the USA is effectively continuing a Cold War with Russia in Europe, as evidenced by the NATO missiles in Poland, it is pursuing an entirely different policy in the Middle East. Cooperation with the Russians was indeed decisive for paving the way to peace in the area. Recent events in the Ukraine that have encouraged the Russophile tendencies we have seen lately in that strategic nation can only stand in the way of the trend towards appeasement between the USA and Russia. This has nevertheless become necessary, and Europe must encourage it or otherwise it will become distanced from Russia. This is particularly true now that Turkey has unwisely taken sides, coming down squarely beside the Egyptian Muslim Brotherhood in an attempt to delegitimise the soldiers who have so far emerged victorious from the civil war in the Germany of North Africa: in other words Egypt.

In this context, Europe, as I have repeatedly pointed out, has more need of Russia than ever. The Gaullist formula of a Europe that stretches from the Atlantic to the Urals is as timely as ever. To achieve this, Putin must nevertheless hasten to overcome the top-down theory and practice of a power that is still overcentralised, the result of a post-despotic control system that still pervades the entire Russian polyarchy, as evidenced by the case of Khodorkovsky and the heavy penalties imposed on those who come out and protest against the powers-that-be. The Russian political system is complex and slowly evolving from the bottom up towards a democratic version of polyarchy, in other words, the interplay between systems of economic interest and territorial representation. A radical reform of the judiciary and an expansion of civil liberties would be decisive steps towards unleashing all of Russia's immense economic potential. Europe needs it: Italy needs it more than ever. Russian interests in Italy have begun to appear on the Mediterranean and could make a formidable contribution to our need for foreign capital. We need the Russians, not only as tourists, but above all as investors, as partners in the field of energy and elsewhere (and here ENI[2] can teach us a lot). We need to fully understand that Europe needs stronger ties with Russia to counterbalance the disproportionate weight of Germany and such ties are also essential for Europe both economically and diplomatically.

The Mediterranean must return to being a sea of peace and this can be achieved by moving away from a balance of terror and returning to a balance of cooperation, in a new Europe that sees North Africa and the Middle East as essential partners. Russia has a fundamental role in this more evenly poised version of the Mediterranean balance. This has been borne out by recent international events, fraught with risk of course, but essential in order to further the process of passive stabilisation. Without strong economic integration and closer diplomatic cooperation with Russia, Europe will be unable to overcome the economic crisis and at the same time help achieve peace in North Africa and the Middle East. In this sense, the sanctions advocated by the USA against Russia are a tragic mistake if they become more than firm diplomatic protests and come to threaten the economic interests of this great country, which will drag all of Europe down with it if it goes into meltdown. In this sense, the energy agreement signed between Putin and Xi Ping is an exceptional event for many reasons. Let us take a look at those reasons in order. The first is geostrategic. Both Russia and China join forces to escape the neo-imperial world view of the USA, which wishes on the one hand to isolate Russia from Europe by means of the Transatlantic Free Trade Agreement, which would create an immense trade area from which Russia would have to be excluded both militarily and economically, effectively neutralising its recent entry into the WTO in 2011.

As far as China is concerned, the Trans-Pacific Pact, with the crux of the military agreement between the USA and Australia coinciding with the inclusion of Vietnam and the exclusion of China from the area of free trade between southeast Asia, South America and the USA should pave the way, with the rearming of Japan, to a kind of boa constrictor hold on the Middle Kingdom. It could be said that Europe has unconsciously backed this neo-imperial design of the USA, as evidenced by the uncertainty and weak response from Brussels over the Ukraine crisis. Russia and China have responded to an exclusive neo-imperial strategy with an inclusive agreement over the economy in terms of energy. This brings us to the next aspect: it is a 30-year agreement with tax breaks for Russia and the provision of 38 billion m^3 of gas per year for an estimated value of approximately \$400 billion per year, even though the prices naturally remain secret. It is a

---

[2]ENI, Ente Nazionale Idrocarburi, leading Italian multinational oil and gas company.

massive agreement that does justice to all the catastrophic illusions that maintain it is possible to work with gas as though a free market as opposed to an oligopoly. This should give the storytellers who have half-destroyed the European energy industry with their pig-headed liberalist ideology plenty of food for thought, all the more so because this is taking place against the backdrop of a deep-seated European crisis throughout the entire sector. For the first time since World War II, one of the countries that is spearheading international economic growth has been affected by the return of something that is technically known as "energy poverty", in other words a growing number of families and microenterprises do not have enough money to pay their electricity and gas bills.

The most surprising news is that the country in question is the United Kingdom, whose leading Thatcherite and post-Thatcherite politicians and intellectuals (headed by Tony Blair) have been standard bearers for energy privatisation as well as liberalisation, from power plants through to nuclear plants and gas production and distribution. The only thing left untouched is North Sea oil. Of course, the ongoing economic recession makes the whole thing more sensational, though what is even more sensational is the fact that the signs of this crisis are spreading throughout Europe. My belief is that the economic sustainability of the entire continental energy sector is seriously at risk. It should be stressed that we are witnessing in Europe—more in some nations and less in others—the closure of gas distribution plants and nuclear power plants due to the fall in wholesale electricity prices and this is having serious repercussions on the continuity of energy supply (and this is coupled with the poverty I mentioned earlier). All this is taking place at the time of a boom in renewable wind and solar power sources that are backed by a policy of state subsidies that have greatly contributed to the fall in prices of fossil fuel energy sources.

As I said, the economic crisis and the increase in poverty naturally accentuate these processes that largely arise as a result of the huge blunders that have been committed for more than 20 years by individual states but mainly by Europe as a whole. I refer to the process of hyper-regulation that has fundamentally depressed investments, thwarting the streamlining of the sector due to the proliferation of brokers who are milking the revenues. This has led to an unprecedented increase in processes of bureaucratisation that have caused skyrocketing costs for production and distribution companies, suffocated by a Soviet-style Gosplan of unprecedented destructiveness. What should have been a mechanism for facilitating the lowering of prices and allowing them to find their own level through competitive mechanisms has instead proved to be a sort of many-headed Leviathan. The biggest of these has grown out of the body of Europe and the Commission. The others are growing out of the bodies of the individual European nations that all have their own regulatory authorities as well as ministers with responsibilities for energy (often competing with one another) who fix the prices and rules of "competition" from the top-down, in hierarchical fashion, creating a gigantic and unwieldy administrative mechanism.

This conjures up a vision of the Black Paintings depicting Saturn devouring his children painted by Goya during his overwrought nightmares and now displayed in the Museo del Prado. The children in this case are the energy companies that are no longer able to make a profit. Not to mention the households of the consumers whose incomes often have to stand the burden of cost increases as well as state subsidies for renewable energies: it is no coincidence that the state does not pay these itself but instead loads them directly onto our household bills. With the never-ending economic crisis, the Giants are gobbling up as many of the poor little people as they can at an incredible rate. And there is more. The boom in shale gas and shale oil in the USA could kill off gas production and distribution in Europe. All the American companies now produce and consume energy at low cost due to the boom, but this is leaving less and less space for the coal market. A solution has been found. New coal markets are being sought in Europe and Asia with a consequent crisis in the prices of traditional energy production and distribution costs. In Italy, these processes are having a radical impact but no one is saying anything about it. Now the problems are likely to become much worse.

The repercussions of this institutional and economic crisis were less severe for the great managerial capacities of the European energy companies, including Russian companies—first and foremost GAZPROM—which are coming up against the ideological hostility of the European technocratic authorities. Lastly, the other significant aspect of the agreement (and it is worth repeating it with regard to my recent comment about coal arriving in Europe) is environmental. In other words, gas is better than coal! Gas does not pollute and allows multiple forms of safe energy efficiency.

When that agreement was made, everyone heard the groans of the President of the European Commission, Barroso, who discovered Russia's strategic role too late and called them to order over supplies to the Ukraine and ultimately Europe (forgetting that, in any case, the amount provided for in the Russian–Chinese agreement represented and still represents 35 % of the annual amount of Russian gas supplied to the whole of Europe, confirming Russia's split European and Asian role...). It was truly a pathetic picture that we did not deserve, we who believe and have believed in the United States of Europe and who believe that if only Europe can have both Russia and the USA as simultaneous allies it can become a world power again. Alongside the USA, of course, which should radically rethink its foreign policy. The fate of the world depends on this. Never before have international economy and politics been so inextricably linked as they are at the moment. And the global recession is tightening these links all over the planet.

BRICS will grow less and at a slower pace, and this will calm growth throughout South America, except in Mexico and Colombia, which have chosen a path that is not so firmly tied to the fast and furious commodity cycle, which incidentally is now collapsing, taking the commodity-dependent countries down with it.

All the other countries will be forced to reclassify the relationships between the mining and oil and gas industries and the world cycle, turning increasingly towards the domestic market as well as towards new foreign markets. This is basically the desire of their middle classes who have become mobilised in recent months and effectively reflect the theories put forward by Tilly, Haimson and myself when we studied the phenomena of collective mobilisation. Such phenomena arise only during ascending phases of the economic and political cycles and impose changes in the agenda of consumption. Now the middle classes of these countries want infrastructures and intangible assets such as culture and quality of life. This leads them to rediscover every tradition (the political cycle) that can lay the foundations for creating their organisational solidarity.

And so we have secularism in Turkey and nativism in some South American countries. This has already taken place and will soon spread more widely: this is the case not only in Bolivia but above all in Peru, the epicentre of all South American political cultures. This will have profound implications on the exploitation of mineral resources, opening a new chapter in the history of South American energy.

The world is now naturally dominated by the North African conflict, which is seeing the return of a form of Nasserism revisited and reshaped by the changes that have taken place on the international front with the fall of the USSR, with the re-emergence of the military as a stabilising force, but not in the same way as in the past. In the case of Nasser and also with Ba'athism, hence also in Syria and in Iraq, they were building the nation: now they are defending it from postdestruction cosmopolitanism of the caliphate (with Ataturk) that has brought the Muslim Brotherhood into being and now endangers their very relationship with the West amongst what remains of that past and the new hierocratic formations that are seeking various ways to assume power—after the fall of the Shah in Persia—throughout the Middle East and in all Muslim areas of the world.

These enjoy the support of powerful state forces, such as Iran on the one hand and Saudi Arabia and Qatar on the other; Saudi Arabia and Qatar, which are in turn engaged in a bitter struggle for hegemony in the Sunni world, which is also reflected in the context of pan-Arab satellite information in the duel between Al

Jazeera, the Qatar TV station and al-Arabiya, which expresses the interests of Saudi Arabia and the United Arab Emirates. All of this has been brought on us by the "Arab Springs" that soon revealed themselves for what they really were and on which I and others have written at length: a revolt of the middle classes, both secular and Islamic, one army against the other. And it is still going on, encouraged by the moral suasion of the USA, which was determined to renew the Egyptian command block that may have been founded on saprophytic soldiers but was still effective in maintaining law and order, against Israel first and foremost.

Lack of understanding of the changes in the Arab, Persian and Turkish world by the USA has been catastrophic, preventing them from evaluating the instability of the institutional roots of the Muslim Brotherhood. It is not enough to have constitutionalised their behaviour, as has happened in Jordan and Morocco (lest we forget, monarchies by divine right, as I have already mentioned, due to their direct descendance from the Prophet!) for approximately 50 years: even all of this has not been enough to govern a country like Egypt or Libya! In overcoming their links with Islamic roots founded on the identity of Islamic law and state law, it has been forgotten that Salafism enjoyed strong support from Saudi Arabia whilst Qatar supported the Muslim Brotherhood.

Replacing the military with those who were believed to be constitutionalised was therefore not enough to transform the system of weights and influence in the Middle East and North Africa. The process of deactivation of military dictatorships by political reform entrusted to forces such as the radical Sunnis has had the same effect seen in Iraq and long before that in Iran, bringing to power the more intransigent Shiism, which is the factor that has now destabilised Lebanon and Syria and holds sway in Iraq. The risk of an all-out "Islamic civil war" fought between Shiites and Sunnis and even within the Sunni world itself is becoming more and more real.

It is important to remember that internal strife has characterised Islamic civilisation from its very beginnings: the first Islamic civil war, known in Arabic as *Fitna* (a term that reflects concepts of divine proof and discord) that emerged following the death of the third caliph Uthman between supporters of the right to succession of one of the companions of the Prophet and those who claimed the rights of his family members (the *Ahl al-Bayt*, "the people of the house") who sided with *Ali ibn Abi Talib*, cousin and son-in-law of the Prophet. The conflict between these two groups around which different socio-economic formations came into being gave rise to the rift between the Sunnis and Shiites which today constitutes the fault line that divides countries that are very different from one another such as Syria, Iraq, Lebanon, Yemen, Bahrain and Pakistan.

Alongside these ancient rifts, deep-seated conflicts are developing with particular virulence within the Sunni world, for example between secularists and Islamists, but also within the heterogeneous and composite Sunni Islamist galaxy itself. The clash of civilisations between Islam and the West feared by Huntington has been replaced by a molecular conflict within the Islamic world that threatens to overwhelm even the nation states, as evidenced by the disintegration of Syria: a tragedy that threatens to strike with particular ferocity the ancient Christian communities of the Middle East, a historical bridge between the West and Islam.

Traditionally, Arab Christians were protected from the Caliphal authorities by giving them the status of *dhimmi*, which admittedly legally sanctioned their subordination to the Muslims but at least guaranteed their lives and their property. The current crisis amongst the precarious Arab nation states, dubbed the "Arab Spring" by the media, is instead causing a proliferation of radical Sunni Islamist movements that see the Christians but also the secularists and Shiites as a cancer to be wiped out at all costs. This profound and agonising crisis within the Islamic world is rampant in the Central African lands, for example in Mali and Nigeria. It even jeopardises the stability of the Congo, which was rebuilt so painstakingly after the war of the Great Lakes and the genocide. The latter paved the way to a territorial partition that has now unusually been entrusted to the African élites, which are negotiating directly with an increasingly intrusive China as well as with the ancient colonial powers, first and foremost France and the United Kingdom.

The realignment of powers in Central Africa cannot fail to come up against the problem of stabilising Nigeria. This nation-building is fundamental to an understanding—and the same applies to the Congo—of what will be the fate of these lands and these cultures. More complicated still is the problem of the entire area that stretches from Morocco and the Gulf to Iran: this constitutes the new battleground of the Islamic world that sees the hegemonic role of the USA distancing itself more and more, with consequences that could be devastating if this vacuum is not immediately filled.

The energy issue is crucial but not enough to understand the situation. Even in 1956—at the time of the war that broke out between Israel, France and the United Kingdom against Nasser, who nationalised the Suez Canal—the USA took the opportunity to replace the decline of British hegemony with an unscrupulous struggle against Soviet influence that saved both Egypt and Israel from ruin.

Now the game is more complicated. Certainly, shale oil and gas are making OPEC increasingly weak, as revealed by the Saudis with their ready denials and phenomenological evidence of rifts in the Royal family: but the opposition to

OPEC is much older. It dates back to when, from the mid-1970s, the proven and unproven reserves began to be concentrated no longer in the hands of the major oil companies but instead in the hands of the NOCs, the national oil companies that were mainly non-OPEC but now hold 90 % of it. This gave rise to a striking technological revolution involving the disintermediation of the same majors who contractualised the disintermediation by selling the NOCs the capabilities to deal with the new technological horizons that were gradually unfolding. This led to an increase in competition and a host of new independent entities in the world energy oligopoly. This exploded with the realisation of the dream of the great George Mitchell who, after years and years of struggle, managed to realise his dream of extracting gas and oil from fracking. He worked on the project throughout his life (1919–2013) with a utopian generosity that has now, alas, disappeared from the international energy world.

Shale oil and gas is nevertheless giving rise to geostrategic macroeconomic and microeconomic changes. The latter are reflected in the transformation of the energy industry, because they have made room for small independent companies due to the number of "wild cat" wells required by shale oil and the plunge in gas prices caused by the shale finds, despite an increase in transport costs that is bound to revolutionise intermobility strategies on a local and global level. Macroeconomically, the role of coal and oil is bound to increase in areas not affected by fracking, because the USA will step up the energy independence that they have achieved by exporting much less oil and gas than they did at one time: all this puts pressure on the price level, downgrading the profit trends of the majors that, despite an increase in extraction and transport costs, are seeing a decrease in the price of oil and gas, due both to fracking and to the ongoing world economic crisis.

The crisis is indeed deepening in the BRICS countries which are most affected by processes of fracking due to their low levels of human settlement. But the most significant consequence is geostrategic, with a consistent loss of interest by the USA in dominating the Gulf area and North Africa and the Middle East in general. A dangerous power vacuum is opening up, but Europe is unable to fill the void due to its internal divisions, the lack of a European army and the devastating consequences of the economic austerity that has destroyed industry in its Southern European strongholds: some of the strong areas are at risk of the collapse of procurement and domestic markets or errors of governance due to the Franco-German divisions, as evidenced by the EADS case.

France's imperial impulses are not backed by sufficient economic force to be supported militarily and economically. Only a Europe that includes Russia could perform the hegemonic task necessary to protect and stabilise—through a combination of military intervention, diplomatic manoeuvring and trade agreements—an area that is destined to be central to the very survival of Europe both from the viewpoint of internal security (due to the possible penetration of terrorist cells that proliferate within the Islamic diasporas due to their all-consuming crises of identity) and due to the potential development of the reservoir of energy present in the area, which is at risk of ending up in the hands of China, a country that may be in decline but is even more dangerously aggressive for this very reason.

The fact that an alliance is emerging between Saudi Arabia, Israel and Russia to bring the Syrian situation under control, supporting Assad and supporting the Egyptian military who saved Egypt and the West from the creation of a huge salaphite Islamic state that could have threatened both Europe and Central Africa is a positive factor: but one enormous hurdle must be overcome before it can be institutionalised. This is first and foremost cultural, due to the fall of the culture of Westphalia and the shameful humanitarian and human rights intervention theories that paid no heed to the cultural compatibility and specificity of the nations, peoples and élites involved. All this plunged the West into an anti-Kissinger backlash and we are only now beginning to assess the enormous prices to be paid. The military break between Shiites and Sunnis is only the beginning of a long inter-Islamic war that we have spoken of previously (continuing the war between Iraq and Iran that we have forgotten all too soon), which can only be resolved by restoring communication between the three fundamental cultures in the area: Arab, Ottoman (now Turkish) and Persian. The West must perform this role. The United Kingdom is best equipped culturally to accomplish this task. Italy has immense untapped resources that it could deploy if only it had the will to do so.

Against this backdrop, however, Italy is falling apart. We are certainly not being pulled up by the lukewarm European recovery, determined by the fact that the economy has to touch rock-bottom before a new cautious rise takes place in the first descending cycle, which will in turn be followed by a new recession with a new reduction in GDP. The fundamental problem is in fact the shrinking in consumption. The organic flow of capital is being cut off, partly as a result of deflation, which shrinks consumption as it lowers profit margins. Incredibly enough, we are still wondering whether or not to cut taxes in this situation!!!

Apart from anything else, the Teutonic austerity is having an impact on Germany itself. Merkel won the election although she was forced into a coalition with the SPD, but the crisis will hit Germany as well. This is because the unequal and cyclical accumulation of capital is stronger than any liberalist–monetarist ideology, even in Merkel's own land. She won the September 2013 elections in her own country, thereby bringing Europe to its knees. The coalition with the SPD will turn the latter into the underdogs and will be devoid of any independent cultural dignity in the face of the liberalist and deflationary policy. I have already said too much about the fact that it makes no sense to allow the Germans to impose their diktat on the entire continent. Only the memory of Paolo Baffi sustains us, in the hope that his words, his writings, will today be re-read and it will be possible to reformulate the entire European constitution accepted by Italy in the fatal illusion that the external monetarist constraint would change the basic face of a nation. A nation where neoclassical and monetarist stupidity is revealed as the harbinger of immense social, moral, cultural and spiritual damage, giving rise to a slaughter of the innocents that was then amplified by financial capitalism just as Minsky predicted. Minksy's work should be read together with the words of Baffi to help us understand what has happened in Italy and in Europe over the past 20 years. It is always the culture that decides the economy, never the other way round.

These days in Italy, despite this situation, people harp on about the government crisis as if nothing had happened. Italy is now truly a state with fragmented powers that is held up by the judiciary against a web of upheavals in our own Constitution. This explains why everyone looks to the great figure of Giorgio Napolitano in this situation of de facto presidentialism that has occurred.

Of course, it is unthinkable for the USA and Merkel (Europe does not come into it, but Germany has powerful and geostrategic interests in areas of the Mediterranean at risk of implosion) that with Egypt and Syria in flames, Italy will collapse into an economic black hole (on the subject of recovery, the Europe-wide data on regional competitiveness that were recently released are evidence of this ...). They cannot let a situation occur, for example, where nothing is done internationally or leave Italy to sink into institutional and social chaos, which would stoke a thousand fires on the prairie. Even in the case of a military intervention in Syria, against Germany's will, the problem would not go away: it would actually become more acute and substantial. Sinai, currently the focus of a violent jihadist insurgency, would become even more ungovernable, as would Syria itself, together with all of North Africa. We would no longer see only the disembarkation on our shores of people who are desperate and humiliated by poverty and terror but also of ideologically and militarily armed cells that would certainly not be content to entrust themselves to a few feeble boats. The coasts of Sicily, Calabria and Apulia would become the extension of a bloody ideological war in a headless state—Italy. This dangerous state of affairs must force us to impose institutional stability. These problems are in truth far more pressing than those of the European Semester, even though this is also very important. Yet again, international intervention is needed before Italian stability can be achieved, as has always been the case in the most tragic and troubled times of our history.

The Old and the New Convergence

The epoch-making events that we have been discussing are a reflection of the end of what I would call "the old convergence", which has now disappeared. I will try to explain the concept. For many decades in economic, and historical and economic analysis, simultaneous growth on a world scale has always been considered to be a convergent process. In other words, we asked ourselves what were the factors that determined—essentially from the twentieth century—a world trend in work productivity, trade and lifestyles that gradually became homogeneous as well as more intense from the periphery to the centre. The convergent growth model broke down a few years ago. Superimposed graphs have been replaced by a fractal pattern of geometries that are variable, mobile, overlapping and quick to appear. It seems there is no longer a peak that can be converged on. Europe is indubitably in a terrible downward slide, militarily, first and foremost, because it was unable to turn the Franco-German armies and those that surrounded them into a new European army.

The world military dominance that is firmly in the hands of the USA is being redefined. This is because the Soviet Union has collapsed and Putin's Russia is less threatening. I even think that European diplomacy believes it to be much more threatening than it really is. This is why North American disengagement in Europe, which is increasingly evident, is accompanied by an economic shrinkage in Europe, which is also increasingly evident and worrying, particularly due to the demographic drop—striking in Germany—that is simultaneously the outcome and the cause of the shrinkage. Hence, the emergence of a fractal or uneven pattern of growth that shows great variation even within the same growth areas.

Growth in Asia, where social and economic situations that are very different from one another combine, is impetuous and often overestimated because too little is known about it.

We are left with the nub of the matter: nowadays a divergence has come about instead of a convergence. If we look at things from a European viewpoint, in other words from the viewpoint of European shrinkage, this clearly diverges from the pattern of Asian growth. I prefer to talk about European divergence from trans-Pacific growth, in other words growth in the area that has the Pacific Realm at its heart and that has seen the United States perform a hegemonic function, unifying billions of people in a trade treaty at one stroke: from the Philippines to Burma, India, Vietnam, Mexico, Peru, Chile, New Zealand and even Australia. The United States have drawn up a military treaty with these nations whose meaning is extremely clear, when we consider that China has been excluded from this major agreement. This is the deeper geostrategic significance of the Trans-Pacific Partnership.

European divergence from world growth emerges strikingly if we view it from the context of trans-Pacific indicators.

But the most striking fractal pattern is that of the United States, whose fate is an enigma. Indeed, as soon as we lift our heads from the statistical data and look at the power of attraction that the North American military and economic machine exercises over all the areas of new growth, we become less certain about that divergence. It is certainly a divergence with a variable geometry, involving military, technological, energy control and capability peaks that continue to advance over every area of new growth. If we consider the role that the United States has again begun to exercise over the past 20 years—by no coincidence after the fall of the Soviet Union—in South America, where the Brazilian juggernaut is now definitely here to stay, we become increasingly uncertain of the North American decline.

But the most striking about-turn has come about in the field of North American oil and gas, which is now extracted under a common law system (lest we forget: I exploit my land without asking anyone for permission as I would have to do under Roman and Germanic law). This is the redefinition in progress in the world gas reserve thesaurus: the former Gulf supremacy is fading before the new pathways opened up by the giant reserves that have recently been discovered: from Canada to North Dakota and South Texas, through French Guyana and Brazil and extending to Perth and all of Oceania.

As we can see, the USA is again in the centre of the new energy power map.

The vector of the new world energy resources is changing: from a transatlantic vector to a transpacific vector.

It extends from the USA to Australia and overturns the price systems and the relationships between energy sources that now offer genuine price-based alternatives: North American coal will be sent to Europe, which will be forced to use it in its power stations to replace the Russian gas that will no longer be competitive. The repercussions on Gazprom are already evident, and the strategic movement of Rosneft towards shale gas, for example, makes the Gazprom crisis all the more striking.

The main elements of the specific European situation with regard to natural gas concern the supply structure. At present, Europe is characterised by a structure of rigid, take or pay agreements on the supply side whilst simultaneously experiencing a difficult period on the demand side that is dictated by the economic crisis as well as by the structure of "renewable energies" in the electricity sector. An overall rethinking is required, including in the light of the most recent developments with regard to shale gas in the United States and elsewhere.

The solution put forward by the European Commission when lobbied by many French and German operators in particular is to set up new import structures for liquefied natural gas (LNG). Of course, the real issue at stake here is different: Where could an LNG operator truly invest in Europe? Moreover, what area of the world is most profitable, at least in theory? Europe is not amongst the most attractive areas, if for no other reason than because it has less appealing prospects in terms of growth volumes and because the margins are less tempting than in other parts of the world. In any case, the idea of a Southern European hub has been doing the rounds for more than 10 years, whilst the northern European countries have in any case already quickly set themselves up with facilities satisfactorily supported by a network of long-term contracts.

This gives the lie to the assumption that it is no longer profitable to invest in Europe (and thus also in Italy). Everything will depend on the formula that will be chosen. We need only think of the Terminal Gate in Rotterdam and the fact that a new terminal is about to enter into operation in Dunkirk in 2015 that will be used only marginally for internal consumption. All these large plants are based on long-term contracts. Having said this, it is important to ask ourselves whether it is more economical to make greenfield re-gassing investments or to extend existing networks. The advisability of entering the European gas market with new energies is dependent on the possibility of drawing up a long-term contract with a major producer that is able to come up with a price that is good enough to beat a proportion of those currently available on the market. This is possible only if we are able to call on a supply that is an alternative to the Russian and Algerian supply but equally powerful in terms of availability and geostrategic influence. One thing that is absolutely clear is that we must change the way we depict our growth model, moving away from one that is symbolised by the highest mountain that is unreachable and far away to one that is symbolised by a chain of mountains, where one peak is certainly higher than the others but no longer unreachable and those who wish to scale the highest and furthest mountain must share the same base camps as those who wish to scale the mountains that surround the highest peak.

LNG—extracted using fracking—is the phenomenological paradigm of a new world geostrategy for the supply of this energy resource, which is becoming more and more indispensable in the light of cultural changes regarding the environment.

Now the price of shale gas must be considered as well as the cultural issue, and the pressure for change is making itself felt more strongly. This is naturally a great transformation that has drawn everyone's attention but in my view it has nothing to do with the recent trans-Pacific agreement mentioned earlier, promoted by the USA amongst some Asian nations and the South American nations bordering the Pacific Ocean.

It is certainly true that the boundaries of world trade are being pushed back. But if we look more closely at matters, trade volumes are not increasing: quite the contrary, from 2006 to 2010 they have fallen constantly, with a dip that was more marked after the world financial crisis in 2007. What has happened? Until 2006, the rate of export growth in Europe and Asia exceeded that of imports and this is because, to that date, sustained demand at world level made it possible to maintain moderate rates of trade. Everything changed after 2007 because the rate of demand for imports fell sharply and simultaneously in the United States, Europe and Japan. From the fourth-quarter of 2008, world trade took a dive: in Europe it fell by 16 %, in the USA by 7 % and in Asia by 5 %. As we know, the world gross domestic product in 2009 plummeted but the contraction in world trade was even stronger. This is the only reason—and one that has eluded most people— why China became the leading world exporter in 2009, overtaking Germany to snatch 9.6 % of the world market.

This was the scenario when, in September 2008, we saw the fall of Lehman Brothers with a drop in property prices and in the value of household assets as well as an increase in saving to the detriment of consumption and investments. The world financial crisis was triggered and had a direct impact on world trade by reducing the supply of credit and knock-on effects due to the reduction in international demand. It could be said that we are facing a strong decline in the sale of all forms of goods that are exchanged in world trade: consumables for immediate consumption, consumer durables and those designed to support investment in machinery and technology. All this causes international trade to plummet.

Households respond to deflationary pressures by not consuming or consuming less. Companies, on the other hand, respond by integrating vertically. In other words, they go back to producing most of the intermediate goods that they need to develop the production chain in-house, as they did during the years from 1950 to 1980. But this means allowing inter-State trade to drop and breaking the international production chains, which are the backbone of globalisation. Companies seek to respond in this way to the credit crisis that has them in its grip but this action has a devastating effect on business-to-business trade and also on trade between banks and businesses, in a kind of local mini autarchy. Lastly, we must also consider that all this has increased the distrust between long-standing world trade partners. All companies respond to the credit crisis by shrinking their international trade volumes. We need only consider that the contraction in world trade (in 2009 it was 12.2 % less than in 2008) has even exceeded the worldwide rate of decline of gross domestic product, which fell by 2.2 % during the same period.

In some ways it is a miracle (and herein lies, so far, the difference between this crisis and the 1929 crisis) that despite everything and unemployment figures of approximately 200 million in the OECD, the States have not yet responded with strong and decisive protectionist policies. Quite the contrary, the current trends I mentioned at the beginning are opposed to protectionism, viz Russia's entry into the WTO and the Trans-Pacific Partnership.

Although the recent appointment of the Brazilian career diplomat Roberto Cavalho de Azevêdo at the head of the WTO, the organisation whose goal is the development of world trade is a very important event that we cannot ignore without making some general observations. In trade policies, Brazil, like Japan, has no compunction about conducting a premeditated currency war and also follows the "principles of the Cambridge School" as they were called back in the day when the economy used to be backed by theories. These date from the 1930s and 1950s and take the form of targeted protectionism aimed at supporting domestic industries and agricultural production based on an economic policy chosen by the government. As we know, these are the principles that, one way or another, with slight variations, are followed by all the BRICS countries despite the military and financial efforts that the USA, in particular deploys in order to change their trade policies.

In the first place, it is highly likely that the trend that has emerged over the past decade in the globalised world of pursuing bilateral trade agreements rather than multilateral agreements will continue, with inevitable consequences on world trade, which will encounter more obstacles and therefore more opportunities to be curbed. Aggregate demand, in other words demand from internal markets, is missing and international demand will reduce in accordance with a fractal pattern with less room for export and the increasing difficulty of always having to find new export niches. In short, the Archimedean point on which the global economy rests is beginning to move from the shoulders of the liberalist giant to the shoulders of the neo-protectionist giant. Of course, there is no need for wholesale neo-protectionism. We would never get out of the recession. But anyone who is aware of world history, especially in Latin America, knows that the first response to crisis has always been *"crecimiento hacia adentro* [inward growth]" and not *"crecimiento hacia afuera* [outward growth]". It is an old story that has now come back into the limelight with radically new aspects: the fact that the nations in question are now medium-sized or major regional powers that the USA will be forced to take into account. Europe will naturally continue to watch from the sidelines.

New conflicting tendencies are therefore in progress and the face of our industrial future, our future as consumers and even our living horizons are still uncertain.

Responding to Strategic Divergences

In this situation the only answer to strategic divergences can come from the recovery of geostrategic leadership. The crisis of political leadership seems increasingly, however, to be a universal phenomenon. It is not a national problem but a geostrategic problem.

We need only think of Australia. This nation is destined to play an extremely important role in the future because the decisive economic and military match with China will be played off in its geostrategic space. The skirmishes formally opened with the Trans-Pacific Partnership between the USA and some Asian states, first and foremost those of the Indochina Peninsula led by Vietnam (China's age-old adversary) and the "Pacific" states of South America: Chile, Peru and Mexico.

Australia teaches us that the antipodal points that lie opposite each other on the Earth's surface, passing through its core, really exist and not only in terms of geography. In other words, there is a focal point extending from the equator upwards to the North Pole through which the vision of the world is completely lost. It is that dimension, facing Europe under the starry sky, that was so magnificently described by Les Murray, the greatest of the Australian poets, when he set out to explain the relationship between Europe and the antipodes by using the analogy of a beautiful painting:

> In the middle of the river are cobweb cassowary trees of the South Pacific, and on the far shore rise dark hills of the temperate zone. To these, at this moment in the painting's growth, my course is slant but my eye is on them. To relax, to speak European.

"Amanda's painting", in Conscious and Verbal, 1999

It is true: a vision exists of the world that the current depression sharpens and makes even clearer: a vision that pushes us beyond our usual generalising preconceptions and makes us see how the geographical, economic and social path that extends from Australia to Africa, through the Indian Ocean, is far more varied than it appears from the top. Consider, for example, and this is obvious from Australia, how the political and social change that has taken place over the past 15 years in Thailand and Indonesia has been decisive for economic development. The first seemed like a pearl of Asian growth, with endless influxes of indirect foreign investment on the financial markets and enviable political stability. Then came the crisis in 1997, the first harbinger of the one that is still going on today: foreign capital withdrew and social problems broke out on the streets. The precarious balance—between the monarchy and the Armed Forces on one hand, and economic wealth transformed into political power on the other—shattered and the country plunged into the de facto dictatorship in which it is now submerged, with continuous clashes between supporters of opposing factions and the collapse of any illusion of guaranteeing this nation—which is central to the geostrategic balance between Laos and Cambodia—a stable alignment.

By contrast, Indonesia, which seemed as though it would never be able to lift itself out of disaster in the slow and ruinous decline it experienced in Suharto's more than 30-year long dictatorship, has achieved remarkable political stability, with the parliamentary dominance of a moderate Islamic party that is guaranteeing a nation of 300 million people a future that seems to be the most serene in all of south-east Asia and Oceania in the broader sense of the word, with profound implications on economic growth marked by interdependence.

All in all, from an antipodal viewpoint, we can still speak of interdependent growth—and not merely interdependent crisis—despite the current world situation. Let us consider one point: the interdependence between economies has certainly struck Australia. This cannot be denied, even though the reductions in GDP are much more limited than our own, heralding a stagnation rather than a depression (the economy is expected to grow about 0.5 % over the coming years if the measures that are being prepared, and that I will discuss shortly, are not imposed). But the fall in Australian exports, for example, which very recently dropped by between 20 and 30 % against Europe and the USA has been offset by an unexpected but very real growth in exports to China, first and foremost of processed coal, which has seen an incredible leap forward. This has come about because the monopolistic capitalist Chinese state has found it impossible to reopen very dangerous, non-economic, small mines that have caused 10,000 deaths at work during the past year alone and has been unable to open new mines despite the presence of huge unexplored reserves that the Chinese do not yet have the technical capacities and economic resources to mine.

In order to meet their energy needs they are importing coal from Australia. I challenge anyone, from a European antipodal point, not to be amazed by this news. China is pursuing a neo-colonial policy all over the world, especially in Africa, but it cannot meet its own bottlenecks in terms of technical and scientific factors and human resources, with consequences that could be severe for its general economic standing.

This is not evident from the North Pole, if you only read the aggregate statistics. And all this is going on whilst battle rages in the arena that has been drawn in the field of the stock exchange and the struggle to buy mining assets from Australian companies. Firstly, the central state issued—one of the first measures taken by the previous Labour government—a list of rules aiming to protect the national interest: no such list existed when the previous Conservative government was in power. Secondly, the Rio Tinto shareholders really do not know what to do in the face of the Chinese purchase offer: they are tempted by the profit they could make due to the immense liquid assets of CHINALCO, which wishes to buy one of the most powerful mining industries in the world, but they are, however, subject to unprecedented political pressure not to sell.

And thirdly, but no less importantly, there are the Chinese themselves, who act with immense political and diplomatic coordination to support the expansionist energy aims. This is achieved not merely through actual occupation of land, as in Africa, but also through action on the financial markets, as in Australia.

And now we come to the most striking thing: the vitality of the Australian stock exchange, even in a period of stagnation and world financial crisis. In the past weeks, the Australian financial market has absorbed more than AU$20 billion through the issue of bonds by the main national corporations who are thus benefiting from confidence in the financial markets that is still very high due to the very transparent and far more prudent attitude adopted by banks in Australia compared to those in the rest of the world, at least to date.

What is really surprising, however, is the strength of national industrial capitalism and the prestige it enjoys in public eyes. Of course, public investment plays its part, but here everything is different. It is the diversity that old growth theorists, who no one reads anymore because everyone is taught in a specialist manner using financial texts, originally taught us to appreciate: we are in a part of the world, here in the Antipodes, where (leaving aside China and India for a moment) Australia is the epicentre of economic areas that often spill over national boundaries due to history, customs and political constructs but that all share a combination of: sparse population and immense wealth in terms of natural resources. We only need reflect that Australia possesses one-quarter of the world's uranium resources to see the thrust of my argument... In areas like this, growth does not rely on a parasite revenue exploitation model—as in many of the oil-producing states of the Gulf, for example—or Nigeria, and I could go on. Growth can be assured only if it is created by distributing wealth in the least unequal manner possible in order to promote the creation of a strong domestic market that is able to shield itself from the inevitable uncertainties and fluctuations of world export flows, which is always possible in a world with economies that are not closed but interdependent.

In short, from an antipodal viewpoint, instability is always present and, unlike in the other hemisphere, invites prudence and not over-reliance on a strategy of risk as has been the case and stubbornly continues to be the case in Europe and the USA. Here in the Antipodes, a world trend that I have already described in my comparison between the ENRON case and the PARMALAT case,[1] the following is becoming increasingly clear: a growing US endorsement of Europe, with collusion of markets and their growing imperfection, contempt for the rules of good governance, reduction in the ability to self-regulate and the continuous creation of inner circles where everyone squares up to prevent any change in those who hold the top positions. Plainly put, we are seeing the disintegration of the establishment, one of the foundations of Western civilisation.

From the Antipodes, everything looks different. We look to Asia, where the evils of capitalist development, which arise intermittently in the USA and continuously in Europe, are inherent in all its various vicissitudes: these may be variegated and distinct, but crony capitalism is the dominant model. Yet things are moving: the fall-off in growth has been weaker than elsewhere, and this is also borne out by what I said earlier about Australian coal and China. Of course, the Pacific Rim, as it was termed by Eric Jones, the great Anglo-Australian economic historian, is separate from everything. Australia does not belong to Asia, to the Asias: it looks out at them, they look at one another. And from this antipodal perspective, we can appreciate that the future match over world domination will be played out on these shores. In other words, the great game will take place to decide whether the impulse for renewal that continues to come out of Australia and New Zealand will be able to tame Asian forms of capitalism and make them

---

[1]See G. Sapelli, Giochi proibiti. Enron e Parmalat capitalismi a confronto, Bruno Mondadori, Milano, 2004

more transparent with less patronage and less dominated by corruption and the threat of violence.

In this sense, the English-speaking Antipodes are really the last outpost for the hope that it is still possible to nurture expectations of and even create in the future a set of nations under a common law that is virtuous not merely because the judges are less imperfect than parliaments but because moral suasion and the civilising influence of Old Europe and particularly the British Empire have not yet faded. If you want evidence of this, we need simply observe how the parliamentary struggle was played out in Canberra—and politically throughout Australia—over the budget. In other words, over the budget proposals that the first Labour government after more than a decade of Conservative rule sought to introduce to deal with the crisis.

Due to the effect on public spending that the government aimed to achieve, the deficit was expected to reach the record sum of approximately AU$58 billion in 2009–2010, without the possibility of returning to a budget surplus for about 5–6 years. This was in the face of a collapse in tax revenue that had already reached the sum of AU$210 billion due to the crisis. The government debt would therefore have to increase to 13.8 % of GDP which, when compared with the figure of approximately 80 % that was expected for other stronger economies in the world, is a true record of health in public finances. The strategy to revive the economy was based on a series of projects to strengthen the infrastructure in a nation where historically the Labour Party, until the era of liberalisation (which was incidentally introduced by the Australian Labour Party before anyone else in the world, long before Blair, on the instigation of Prime Minister Hawke, a powerful trade union leader), was the quintessential advocate of production culture and nation-building.

Now they were reclaiming that culture and that history with their plans to invest AU$22 billion in roads, railway lines, ports and broadband networks for Internet connections. They also planned to make considerable pension increases to revive the domestic market, to slash taxes on small- and medium-sized enterprises and make cash transfers to extended or single-person households. And naturally, there was plenty of support for alternative energies. The most innovative measures, when viewed from the other antipodal pole, our own European pole, are those that aimed to bring about a reduction in spending on civil service salaries, which are expected to undergo cuts that have not been properly specified but are bound to be swingeing and have already given rise to not a few protests—and expenditure of approximately $5 billion, that has already been earmarked, to increase the quality of public hospitals and increase free long-term care for cancer patients, who represent a very sensitive issue here.

Above all, it is planned to increase spending on tertiary education by $5.5 billion: universities and research centres... This really is a surprise: here, people can look to the future. The people that will lose out, according to the Conservative opposition—they are not wrong and the government would be the last to deny it—will be those who are waiting to retire, because the retirement age will rise to 67 for all. The other people who will lose out are those who pay for private health insurance out of their own pockets in addition to the universal public health care because they will no longer receive the very small tax break that they used to get. According to the interpretation of the Conservative government, this is used to compensate them for the reduction in the tax burden on the state: this measure will affect the vast majority of Australians.

The tax-free threshold, in other words the income level below which taxes are not paid, will also increase by about $5000: it will be $25,000 per year for the under 50s and $50,000 for the over 50s. Taxes will also increase for those who earn more than $150,000 per year. The Conservative opposition insisted that these measures will not reduce unemployment and protested over the abolition of tax relief for those who also had private health insurance, suggesting a tax on smoking instead (whilst the government was defeated in Parliament over the idea of increasing taxes of alcohol) but could not in fact offer an alternative to the government of Kevin Rudd and then Julian Gillard, who took over from Kevin Rudd only to be ousted by him again a few months before the elections in September 2013. Politics is a personal struggle wherever you are in the world.

Of course, the Conservatives won the elections and now everyone is waiting to see what changes they will make to the geostrategic situation in Australia. It is highly likely that they will seek a dangerous rapprochement with China throwing all caution and limits to the wind, threatening the very existence of the nation. The restriction of measures on migration, which are already very severe here, is inevitable and already minutely planned. These will have a very heavy impact particularly on potential well-qualified migrants, the aim being to defend the employment market for those who already work in these sectors in Australia. The crucial factor in this situation, however, is not simply how these measures will tackle the crisis. In this context, it is essential to look at a forecast, which was set out in a White Paper that I found to be truly explosive, published by the Australian Ministry of Defence four years ago. This bulky and very detailed study, drawn up with an impressive scientific rigour, argued that from 2014 up to 2030, a staggering AU$25 billion a year would be necessary to rearm Australia in the face of the military threat posed by China, which Rudd, who has a long diplomatic career and who speaks excellent Chinese, believes is determined not to halt its territorial ambitions at Taiwan alone. Taiwan, which Australia incidentally already considers to be part of present-day China, supports the view that there is only one China in the diplomatic arena.

The publication of the White Paper sent ripples through public opinion in Oceania, where people have been discussing the Chinese influence for years, and elsewhere. For example, the Fiji Islands, where a military dictatorship is in place, have long been the target of massive investments and attention from China (Chinese "aid" has gone up from AU$1 million in 2005 to AU$167 million in 2007), as is incidentally the case in all the islands of the Oceanic archipelago. As I was saying, publication of the White Paper sent ripples through all Asian diplomatic circles, reigniting a debate that for years was thought to be over and the echoes of which, albeit only faintly, have reached Europe (and even the USA). This debate focused and still focuses on what we must expect from the growth of China as a great power that aspires to a role that is global rather than regional, even though it does not yet have any of the resources to achieve this.

The first intimation of the resumption of the debate, moreover, occurred during the deployment of naval forces that China proudly and with great fanfare recently unveiled by parading them before the rest of the world in characteristic Middle Kingdom fashion, just as the USSR used to do, as though it were a great power with world hegemonic aspirations. Now Chinese demographic power backs the manifestly true nature of that regime: a military dictatorship that is not afraid to reveal itself. It is nevertheless a dictatorship that holds, and in this it differs from all the other dictatorships in history, a powerful force within it: the often shrewdly managed creative growth of the new middle classes and new forms of political integration that continually compensate for the very severe problems of social cohesion caused by inequality, starting in rural areas and medium-sized industrial towns.

On the international front, however, China behaves like a dictatorial military state, exporting forced labour and state capitals in a composite relationship between monopolistic state capitalism and a return to a strategy of territorial domination with settlement colonies. For this reason, dissent is growing as well as opposition against its conduct primarily in Asia and Africa, where it has more of a stranglehold. Now dissent is also growing from our antipodal pole, which has a different relationship with China to that of any other part of the terraqueous globe. From this standpoint, the trip that Hillary Clinton made to Peking, which was her first trip following her appointment, was seen as an act of unpardonable weakness. In fact China cannot rid itself of the burden of the USA's public debt because this burden enables it to survive in the crisis. We may consider, for example, that the Chinese dragon cannot feed its people without cooperating to create a modern industry that it currently does not possess and can only be given to it by the capitalist West. Everything you see every day comes from Australia and New Zealand: here, it is not a matter of competing with China: it is a matter of working with, for and in China.

The crisis from which the USA is very far from being able to free itself looms worryingly in the face of Chinese power. Obama finds himself faced with a very difficult situation. The current recession played a decisive role in winning him a second term. And the industrial and agricultural forces of the North American giant must now perform a crucial role. This message emerging from the antipodal point running through the same vein of ethnocentrism and geostrategic North Americanism is very specific. We must build a world order that can face up to growth by the Chinese, whose objectives are unstable and uncertain. The USA will only be able to face up to the challenges posed by the economic crises and the clear emergence of China in the world scenario if it re-forges strong links with Russia and Oceania as well as with India, as it has actually already attempted to do.

This is not a paradox, global economic recovery can take place only through the recovery of the North American economy within a framework of cooperation with Russia, which is slowly emerging from the collapse of the USSR, and with the medium-sized Oceanic powers as well as with Japan. This is the reason why international cooperation for a new world order that looks to the Oceanic compass to describe a growth scenario in south-east Asia and not only in Oceania is the decisive challenge that awaits the world. Europe will have to understand that, when faced with this scenario, it must find a unity that currently seems impossible, with the growing breaches between France, Germany and the United Kingdom (even more so if the British Conservative party wins the next elections). Under Les Murray's starry sky, Europe does indeed seem to be a meteor that has lost its way... This is glaringly apparent when viewed from the Antipodes.

The Challenge to Fossil Fuels and the Crushing of Convergent Growth

In any case, this is something that we have learned from the world fossil fuel industry.

It is strange to think that until about halfway through the 1970s, the USA was the largest producer and consumer of oil in the world. A unique case of energy self-sufficiency given the fact that in those days gas did not have the extraordinary importance that it has now assumed. Most of the Western world did not, however, have that oil self-sufficiency.

All countries had to search for oil outside their own borders. Oil is extracted in the same way as gas from the bowels of the earth and then transported and refined from Borneo to London, from the Arctic Circle to Amsterdam—and Rome.

The gas industry is a world oligopoly that survives through cooperation between nations: we can only transport it in various forms if we can purchase it from the nations who have their own gas and only if they decide to sell it to us because that sale does not affect their own power interests. It is undoubtedly a matter of price. In the world today, with North America's conversion to shale gas, the option of liquid transport and the re-gasification network, there are now fewer refineries than 30 years ago in the days of oil—although two giants, China and India (where all the new refineries operate due to environmental legal issues), are huge consumers and very poor producers. In this scenario, a world oversupply of gas is building up, with consequences that may be unprecedented given that this technological revolution coincides with a world recession. Obama's recent unexpected decision to allow the export of oil and gas extracted using shale methods reflects the crisis in which the USA is still mired from the viewpoint of manufacturing, not of services, with serious consequences for the European gas market as well as the Asian market.

Investments are communicating vessels. If they do not communicate, prices go up. If vessels communicate due to investments, prices fall.

Shale gas has now spurred immense investments, building from scratch a worldwide gas industry that is different from the one we used to have, to the point of causing a deep rift within OPEC between the Saudis and everyone else (arguments take place over oil, but problems also arise outside OPEC...).

Crucially, the world axis is shifting ever more towards cooperation in the global gas industry. And this is happening despite the fact that globalisation is changing pace. It is no longer the linear path without contradictions that could be seen after the fall of the Soviet empire, the quiet emergence of China as a balancing power as envisaged by Kissinger (compare and contrast his very recent *On China*...) and the developing of a market where democracies would inevitably be built where the market itself needed it most. In other words, in the Gulf States, in central Asian markets, imitating the democratic and economic stability achieved in Latin America. Except that everything went and is still going differently: the market is admittedly developing but amidst a thousand rifts and cracks and we are suddenly powerfully reminded of Steve Rokkan's forgotten theory of the cleavages that afflict the whole world during processes of change. Before, we had terrorism. Now we have terrorism sitting in a fault line that threatens to divide the world in the area of crisis at the greatest risk of disintegration: the place where the densest fossil fuel energy reserves on the planet can be found.

A fault line that runs through North Africa, splitting it in two, and stretches up to the Persian Gulf, threatening to break through the Middle East and Central Asia like tearing a taut cloth. At one end of this lies Saudi Arabia and its Sunni hegemony threatened by Qatar; at the other end Iran and its Shiite ideology: both divide unevenly, shatter, opposing all the States of the Gulf and of the Middle East, from Lebanon to Persia. Syria is breaking up violently and this rift threatens to engulf even the Hashemite monarchy that reigns over Jordan as well as exacerbating the never-dormant sectarian conflicts in Iraq and Lebanon, naturally threatening Israel. Jordan and Morocco, together with Saudi Arabia, are the "sacred bodies" of a world based on very sensitive balances resulting from the stabilising role of Syria but also due to the decisive role played by the Egyptian army (Egypt used to be known as the Germany of North Saharan Africa).

This has been eloquently demonstrated by the unfolding of the political crisis caused by the mass mobilisation of young middle-class people with no future who acted out the drama of the "Arab Spring".

The Libyan crisis is an indirect result of this general process, with evident differences due to the absence of the State and nation-building conducted by that tribal grouping dominated in Bonapartist manner by Gaddafi after the collapse of the Senussi monarchy. A tribal balance in full disarray has yet to be stabilised and can only be rebuilt by Western powers.

The Anglo-French military pact forged at that stage must be read in this light, in comparison with relative Western military disengagement on the part of the United States.

That pact is effectively a harbinger of the military and strategic development of a combat strategy, which is not European but duopolistic, to control the real object of future contention: sub-Saharan Africa. The Great Lakes region is Conrad's heart of darkness and the future source of power, food and industry. Surrounded by the States that crown the new Congo after "Africa's first world war" that was specifically fought to redefine the Great Lake region post-colonially, the Congolese issue will become the issue of the future. And we must contain the conflict with China, which is already very active and with penetration strategies that are completely different from the colonial strategies of old and the post-colonial strategies of today. This is why the topic should be examined with great care. The next 50 years of world economic history will be the story of the emergence of Black Africa: whoever exercises dominion over those lands together with the Africans will rule the world.

Mali is a former French colony that has been independent since 1960. It boasts a very ancient imperial tradition and is one of the most culturally developed areas of sub-Saharan Africa, in other words the set of States that stretch from Senegal on the shores of the Pacific to the Horn of Africa on the shores of the Indian Ocean. In Europe, we have been so busy waiting with bated breath every day to see what will be decided about the crisis that we never remember that this area of the world houses the largest resources of non-ferrous minerals in the world and immense reserves of oil and gas. We forget that every upheaval in one of these "nascent States" has an impact on all the others.

Mali, with its 15 million inhabitants—80 % of whom are Sunni Muslims and the rest effectively animists—is bordered by Algeria to the north, Niger to the east, Burkina Faso and the Ivory Coast to the south, Guinea to the south-west and Senegal and Mauritania to the west. Its strategic importance is immediately clear: it is the gateway to Black Africa. And the antechamber is the "Libyan" Fezzan that the French have always sought to control. Their way has always been blocked by the "blue men of the desert": the Touareg who claim their independence from Mali. One of the reasons that led to France's intervention in Libya was the control it was able to more extensively exercise over regions such as Mali and beyond through the war. On 22 March, the international correspondents announced that a military coup had been pulled off by the troops of a well-armed but poorly paid army: the Malian army. An army steeped in a nationalism that simmers particularly strongly in the most numerous ethnic group, the Bambara (whose language is, together with French, actually the country's national tongue), who have been fighting the Touareg for centuries and believe that interventions by the central government have been too feeble.

The Touareg want independence and do not hesitate to seek the support of Algeria at all times and effectively hold to ransom the mining companies operating in the area. The Touareg were the most loyal supporters of Gaddafi,[1] to the bitter end. Besides, their family and tribal network extends to Niger, a country that played and still plays a central role as an area behind the power lines of Gaddafi's tribes. The rebels have now deposed President Amadou Toumani Touré, who is barricaded in the capital Bamako, protected by troops loyal to him. The leaders of the revolt (prominent amongst them Captain Amadou Sanogo, who claims to have been trained by the Marines) say they want to return to civilian rule as soon as the Touareg revolt has been crushed. It is also true to say that a separatist attempt is taking place here, as is also incidentally the case in Libya.

This fragmentation worries the big companies working in the region, first and foremost Rangold Resources, which is a genuine inter-State power that expressed strong concerns over the fall of Gaddafi in Libya, fearing chain reactions amongst the various ethnic groups and different tribal powers in the south of Libya. The prophecy came true. Yet now, unexpectedly, we are trying to debunk and forget about the prophecy: cue the appearance of General Khalifa Haftar, who arrived from the deep cocoon of the USA, where he had lived out the previous 20 years in exile in Virginia. He returned to Libya in May 2014 to launch the Karamah ("dignity") operation aimed at defeating all the Islamist militias in battle and forcing the government in Tripoli to accept a programme founded on armed control of the area. The General announced his return from Tunisia and he is clearly supported by the new Egyptian military leader Abdul Fattah al Sisi, who has a strong power-base in Cairo, even though he lost a lot of his credibility, even compared to the Egyptian secular opposition, during the elections in May 2014 that attracted a turnout of only 20 %.

But back to Mali and its emblematic crisis. Naturally, the neighbouring States, joined in an inter-State association without powers of intervention—ECOWAS—and

---

[1]Along with the Qadhadhfa, Gaddafi's own tribe, the Warfalla used to be especially powerful.

the European Union with its glaring inanity, confirmed their support for the deposed president, which could even lead to the military situation being resolved in his favour.

We are nevertheless left with one unresolved question: how to stabilise an area that is likely, now that Gaddafian power is no more (this is the reason why it is always essential to keep abreast of events in Libya), to explode into a thousand fragmented identitarian realities, stretching as far down as the Congo, where unsurprisingly fighting has broken out again on the Rwandan borders? It seems that the stack of dominoes that was once held together by autocratic but not Islamist regimes in North Africa is slowly collapsing with the fall of Libya, pulling down with it as it unravels the power systems that stabilised after the "War of the Great Lakes" that 10 years ago brought peace and "normality" to the new Congo. In these cases too, as in Iraq and in Afghanistan, armed intervention proves to be a harbinger of serious unforeseen consequences, deceiving all those who thought that the use of weapons would solve all problems.

The Future Will Be African

Mali shares a border with Niger, and Niger is the gateway to what remains of the great former Belgian Congo, divided, battered and marked by new conflict as it is. The break-up of Libya, with the sinking of the Fezzan and Sinai in the chaos after the fall of Gaddafi and replacement of Mubarak's soldiers by the Muslim Brotherhood, has meant that the entropy and disorder have spread like wildfire beyond the boundaries of the great Sahara deserts. I feel as though I am reading Hegel's sublime pages on the construction of the European States, a construction that seemed to the great philosopher at the beginning of the nineteenth century, uncertain and extremely difficult. That is all the more true for Africa, you may say. And you may also say so nothing is new? But actually a great deal is new.

The weak formation of new African states is now threatened by a very scary stateless enemy that knows no boundaries. I am referring to the new imperial project supported by radical Islamist movements, which overcomes everything with ultra-high-tech technologies and a supranational geostrategic vision that has been unknown in Africa for the past two centuries. Those who took on the infidels that destroyed Gaddafi's Libya and threaten to overflow if Alawite Syria should fall are now the supporters of a new African post-colonial imperial regime: they are the radical, Salafi and jihadist radicals of various sects that, if Mali were to be occupied, would expand more rapidly to the West, towards Algeria and Niger, to the south, towards Burkina Faso and Nigeria and then on to the Congo. The problem is the control of the entire continent's energy resources by the new—de facto—Islamic caliphate of Central Africa, together with China, which has not yet decided who to side with. The attack on the plants shared by BP (British), Statoil (Norwegian) and Sonatrach (Algerian) is not at all or at least not only a retaliation against Algeria's decision to allow French aircraft to fly over Republican territory, but a specific symbolic action indicating the reclaiming of African energy resources by the neo-Islamists.

Everything has indeed changed with the emergence of armed political Islamism. The Europeans have noticed, although the news has necessarily been muffled. Even Germany, always so hostile to military engagement, has wasted no time in this case in aligning itself with France, with its long experience of war in the heart of Africa. The energy resources of the African giant are rightly seen as crucial to growth, or rather to future survival.

Italy must also accept that this is the end of an era. We can no longer conduct post-colonial African politics as we did in the old days, forging links with dominant African groups. Nowadays, even the power of the neo-clanist and post-tribal organisations is challenged by a geostrategic and political player of a type that we have never known before in Africa: radical political Islamism that does not limit itself to territorial control (Somalia, Sudan, etc.) but aspires to a supra-national neo-caliphal dominion that upsets the extremely fragile inter-State relations that have been built up with such great effort in Africa over the past two decades.

This battle must therefore be fought using different strategies, without ever being able to rule out war, armed struggle, as has long been understood by the French and the English-speaking world in the guise of the vacillating states of Rwanda and Burundi from where the attacks on Kabila's Congo originate. Italy, a medium-range Mediterranean power, cannot fail to make its voice heard, even if that means militarily, or it will be forever excluded from Black Africa and from the new Africa that is building up from the Mediterranean to the South Pole. A lot of spending is necessary, with a radical rethinking of European budget constraints. Everything is within our power: an excellent military and paramilitary industry; young scholars who are keen to learn and understand. But we must revise our political thinking. We would be well-advised (after the 2014, European elections campaign, naturally, so as not to get in the way of the political wheelers and dealers) to begin to do so with courage and conviction if we do not wish to compromise our future forever.

The great fault lines of history, between the Mediterranean, Persian Gulf and the Indian Ocean, have always been decided by meeting or collision, now tougher than ever, between the three great civilisations that have dominated those lands for centuries: the Arab, the Persian and the Turkish. Only the collapse of the Ottoman Empire obscured this truth, with the treaties signed back during World War I that led to the creation of a set of States that had nothing to do with either ethnicity or history. States without a nation: herein lies the Arab problem.

The other side of the coin is nations with strong States, built by a modernising élite: herein lies the secret of Persian tradition and Turkish invention. This balance could only be sustained because Europe was otherwise engaged between the two world wars laying the grounds for the destruction of the Treaty of Versailles, including the treaty establishing the Kurdish state drawn up on paper at Sèvre and destroyed by the Kurdish factions themselves a couple of years later. Immediately after World War II, two bulkheads were built against Stalinism: in the East, Saudi Arabia, a North American construct between tribalism and sacred dominion of religious tradition; in the West, Egypt which, after the USA broke with much fanfare from post-colonialism movements to conquer the nationalised Suez Canal, was intended to be, with Sadat, the faithful guardian of North African Atlanticism after the decline of the former British hegemony in the Mediterranean.

Everything was strategically joined together, albeit by opposing fronts, in a single strategic movement that was not in fact divided, as most people think, by the Cold War. This gave meaning to Turkey's role as NATO's southern flank and made it possible to establish a balance of power in Syria too. And the elder Assad succeeded magnificently in this. I had the opportunity to meet him and he made a lifelong impression on me. This came about due to the Alawites "created" by France and strongly supported by the USSR and the Christian churches in the stated intention of moderating Baathist extremism that, as we realised after the end of the USSR and the destruction of secular nationalist alternatives to both Westernism and communism, unfortunately flooded out in a kind of localist neo-imperialism that culminated in the Iran–Iraq conflict, which raged for no less than 10 years. The fall of the Shah and even earlier the unfortunate fall of Mohammed Mossadegh due to an Anglo-American coup that was as foolish as it was ill-conceived, paved the way, years later, for a hierocratic machine, the like of which had never been seen either in Iran or in the Arab and Turkic world.

In this context, neo-Islamist terrorism in a jihadist mould calls into question, to my mind, the great international breakthrough that developed throughout the 1990s. Just as globalisation opened up financial markets to a lamentable lack of regulation, the abandonment of a firmly Westphalian Kissingerian view paved the way for a series of military forays without any strategic thought that led to a black hole of international disorder over the last two decades. A hasty, patchy and sectarian reading of Leo Strauss, who knew everything about the Bible but nothing about Machiavelli (Hegel's words against Frederick II, a critic of Machiavelli, would have come to mind had not the tragedy turned into farce) did the rest.

Just as the absence of regulation unleashed the most terrible financial crisis of the past three centuries (that only Hyman Mynski foresaw), intellectual followed by diplomatic overturning of Westphalian concepts of foreign policy stormed onto the world stage, overturning all the mechanisms of weight and relevance that had built the world order in accordance with a Kissingerian strategy of world trilateralism: China, USSR, USA. Europe had always been missing from this design, because the plan hatched by Adenauer and De Gaulle never came to fruition and the efforts by Mitterand and Kohl to follow through the Élysée Treaty, the fiftieth anniversary of which was celebrated in 2013, dried up over the role of the strike force and the effective absence of a British interlocutor able to offset, with France, the overbearing weight of Germany in a Europe that was at that time dominated by the Cold War.

Then, people who had never voted were called upon to vote not in accordance with territorial representation, but in accordance with lineage, strength and chaos wreaked with the intention of declaring winners and establishing leaders, or doing so through corporate instead of personal power. And so we saw new beginnings (as in Ukraine and Georgia, new beginnings that only the pen of the Italian cartoonist Arbasino or the cartoonists of the New Yorker could do justice to, they are so nauseating and fake... except when they become tragic and dramatic when one of the humiliated oppressed sets himself on fire and the flames rage on the Prairie...).

What is happening in Africa today, firstly in the north and then gradually extending out towards Black Africa, is primarily the outcome of failure to stabilise transatlantic relations between Europe and Russia. We should not forget that this is a Russia that, after the fall of the USSR, was humiliated and strategically isolated between Europe—with missiles trained and unwavering anti-Gazprom liberalist policy on one hand—and an aggressive and increasingly well-armed China on the other side of the Urals. The Gaullist idea of a Europe from the Atlantic to the Urals was the only international counterweight that could offset what now amounts to, without Europe and without the no-longer-Communist Russia, the USA going it alone in a world situation that sees the great North American nation reaching out to its Asian destiny or rather its Pacific destiny (in the Pacific Realm). But instead—despite the fact that it will be the leading energy power in the world by 2020—it must hang on to guarantee the energy sources indispensable to its lazy, tired and cowardly European ally, that is unable to find itself and build a self-sufficient military force that can guarantee safety, not the peace that means nothing at all, on the southern flank of NATO and in North Africa.

France has grasped the problem. It still has what is needed these days: an imperialist mentality or culture! From this point of view, the collapse of Egypt was a disastrous event. Only the foolishness and ignorance of an intelligence system now devoid of the outstanding intellectual qualities that it once possessed could ever have thought that Morsi's Muslim Brotherhood would be able to replace Mubarak once Russia had been removed from the list of strategic allies, not of Egypt but of stability in the area. No, Russia must be humiliated and weakened in Syria, a Russia weakened and humiliated by North American mistakes.

Russia is suffering from a strategic isolation that stops it from exercising the role of moderation, intelligence and mediation that it has always exercised, once British hegemony ceased in the Mediterranean, to be replaced by that of the USA. The role of the USSR was decisive in maintaining balance in the Mediterranean and throughout Africa even throughout the bloody wars for control of the Congo, which involved the Cubans and in any case held Islamist extremism in check. With the collapse of the Soviet Union revealing the humiliation of Russia and its strategic isolation, the USA embraced the dictates of post-Westphalian democratic interventionism that have proved disastrous, even more so when amplified and magnified by the monstrous events of 11 September (as Allan Bloom, who had sadly passed on by then, would have said, it was the only response that was not possible but intellectually conceivable by the American mind ...).

The only thing that Russia is still interested in today is having permanent access to the warm waters, in other words maintaining its Mediterranean base of Tartus in Syria and thus being able to sell the gas and oil without which its economy would not exist. If this is threatened, the entire world balance is in danger. North Africa was and is the first test of this imbalance in the relationships of power that led the USA to an illusion of self-sufficiency and both strategic and military omnipotence. Nowadays, Russia's strategic isolation prevents any containment of the aggressive impulses of all the medium-range regional powers that are currently able to perform a role that is really beyond their capabilities, but made possible by a strategy of containing the ever-precarious breakdowns in the North and Central African area.

This situation is exemplified by Turkey, which pursues neo-Ottoman imperialist designs and endangers the military pact with Israel, which was one of the archetypal balancing strengths in the area and stemmed from the pact, perpetuated through the stabilising role of Syria, further perpetuated through neutralisation of the Palestinians due to the policing role played by the Hashemite monarchy in Jordan and ultimately culminated in Egypt with Mubarak's iron armed grip over Sinai. Now everything has been challenged by the greediness of the army who are nonetheless currently proving themselves to be irreplaceable. Egypt has been abandoned by the USA in its historical construct of power because it was believed that the vacuum left by the USSR would allow a changing of the guard amongst Mubarak's greedy supporters and the established Muslim Brotherhood, who would take over the former's power without affecting Egyptian secularism.

This means that they understood nothing about change in the symbolic Islamic continent. The Muslim Brotherhood have an extremely long tradition of ingenuity, patience and cunning tactics. Their testing ground in Jordan made them capable of an operation to penetrate the institutions without at the same time losing their nature of a mass movement—and like all mass movements they retain great diversity and embrace a range of political spirits. They also maintain the ability, as we are taught by the works of Gerald Bronner, to be open for discussion, development, implementation and carrying forward extreme ideas to the most incredible conclusions, for the very reason that the Muslim Brotherhood, like the Salafists and the jihadists, are not dispossessed; they are not the starving of the Earth, in the third world rhetoric that lingers on in today's world, but sophisticated intellectuals, engineers, experts, entrepreneurs, professionals and networkers with many faces, as the experience of Bin Laden shows us.

The collapse of Gaddafi and Mubarak has moved the balance of geostrategic power in Africa downwards. If Assad falls, it will be an incalculable disaster due to the proliferation of wars and terrorist acts that will ensue, given that entire areas of the country are already controlled by jihadist groups. We will be speaking not of spring, but of the most horrendous winters. There are weapons, trained troops such as the Touareg, interracial conflicts, inter-European conflicts (we need only think of the conflict around the Great Lakes between the French, British and North Americans). There are coup attempts in Eritrea and Ethiopia and movements of troops and armies that are armies by name only and must be supported, armed and led by European and North American powers.

In Africa, it is also essential to go on the ground. There is no room for any Rumsfeld doctrine. The supranational design of the jihadists and Salafists and the increasingly enigmatic and mysterious role of Saudi Arabia, which—lest we forget—is willing to do anything to destroy Iran and eradicate Shiism everywhere, open disturbing questions about the future. Or we could go back to the Peace of Westphalia, intervening only in the case of attack on the energy sources that belong to all of us and transcend property rights—the only possible strategy and one that must be pursued through agreement between the African Union, Europe and Russia and the USA and China (a silent yet ever-present partner that has yet to reveal its cards) by setting up a rapid reaction force that is technologically highly advanced and equipped with very sophisticated intelligence—or we run the risk of chasing after a proliferation of countless local wars and genocides such as those between the Hutus and Tutsis that are already about to break out in many areas of the continent.

For Europe, this would mean quickly establishing a European army and a reappraisal of all the agreements concluded up to now. Everything must be rebuilt. Maastricht and Lisbon and all the rubbishy cronyism of Brussels must be stripped away and mothballed to rebuild a lean, mean, intelligent structure that supports a powerful European army. Public debt will skyrocket as it did during the Hundred Years War. Afterwards, great economic development ensued, with the demographic revolution. The best thing that can possibly be done to put an end to the suicidal policy of austerity. Hydrocarbons and the ways of ensuring they can be reproduced and distributed throughout the world still blaze the trail to progress and overcome the ideologies of the arrogant learned scholars, who are not really learned at all.

All this is taking place in a context in which the decline of North America is not as inevitable as some think, but it is currently thrown into sharper relief than before due to the economic crisis and the strategic uncertainties faced by that great power, which must once again choose at any cost to lead the West. Of course, it is missing the European transatlantic relationship that is essential to guarantee world order. The USA must find another strategic pillar to flank them: Europe can no longer do it in unity. Hence, the importance of confrontation with China and a strategic alliance with emerging countries wish to continue on the virtuous path of globalisation. All this creates a taut, strong, continuous current of unrest around the world.

Consider, for example, what I have been trying to explain of what is happening in the Middle East.

In this global context, must the USA, despite the fact that it will be the leading energy power in the world by 2020, linger on to guarantee the multiple power bases essential to its lazy, tired, cowardly European ally, which is unable to rediscover itself and build a self-sufficient military force that can guarantee safety, not peace, which means nothing at all, on the southern flank of NATO and in North Africa?

How long will the United States, now freed from the need for the transatlantic relationship that ensures control of the Gulf, continue to perform the role—that reaches to the Mediterranean and Israel—of protecting that amazing institutional-North American tribal-Sunni construct that is Saudi Arabia? This is the most dramatic of the questions that strategic thinking faces us with at present.

Thinking of simultaneous growth on a world scale as a convergent process was an essential element of any geostrategic approach to world history, before any other consideration. Everything hung on this point. We asked ourselves what factors led essentially from the twentieth century onwards to a global world trend of work productivity, trade and lifestyles that gradually became not only more homogeneous but more and more intense, from the outside in. This interpretive model was also a reflection of the one that led Ricardo to wonder about decreasing returns and how to stop this decline by gradually expanding new cultivated land.

This model was transposed from Britain to Europe where the "peaceful conquest" (to use Pollard's words) of industrialisation had crossed the Channel and had come to settle over the three Europes like a patchwork cloth: Scandinavian, mainland and southern Europe. Overseas, the United States had taken its own native step towards industrialisation, generating a very specific and particular model that proved so convergent with the British and European model that it actually outstripped it in terms of the wealth produced.

Later, as already mentioned, after World War II, questions began to be asked about possible growth convergences. The starting point was not economic but political, namely the Bandung Conference of non-aligned countries which saw the emergence of two future territorial giants, namely Egypt and India, as growth protagonists. Growth in regimes based on monopolistic capitalism in dictatorial states, in other words countries under "real socialism", was not considered except to demonise it or extol its virtues. This process is repeated today with China and will disappoint followers of that model, embodied in China as a terrorist version of Asian despotism, just as those who sang the praises of the Soviet Union will be disappointed. What counts in each case is emphasising the fact that the stress was on convergence. Towards what? Towards a mixed economy of European countries and the United States with its less mixed economy and more extensive market.

It is no coincidence that these thoughts about growth took place against a backdrop of the international dominance of capitalism and the military might of the English-speaking peoples: first the gunboats and flags of the United Kingdom, followed by the aircraft carriers and flags of the United States. The changeover from one form of leadership to another was effectively immediate and without too many contradictions between those who left and those who took up the baton, with the exception of the conflict that took place between the United Kingdom and the USA during the campaign in Egypt when Nasser nationalised the Suez Canal: the French, British and Israeli parachutists were not accompanied by the North Americans, because the USA wished to repeat with the Egyptian giant the knight's move it made in 1945 in Saudi Arabia to the detriment of the United Kingdom, in other words trading military support for a reliable, long-lasting energy supply.

Rather than energy, Egypt provided a bulwark bolstering North American hegemony over the Gulf states to counter the dangerous hegemonic intentions of the Soviet Union. It had everything: military leadership, economic leadership with Europe in a supporting role and the former colonial countries, with India to the fore, converging towards the English-speaking and European peaks. As Kissinger tells us in his *On China* even Mao and Chou En-lai aspired to converge towards those peaks and not towards the Soviet peaks. This was already clear from the history books, particularly in North America: now we know the story from the lips of the only twentieth-century intellectual who saw his theories implemented on a world scale and has now released transcripts of the talks he was involved in, especially with the giant Chou En-lai. These have been preserved due to the prodigious work of the North American intelligence desk officer who had the job of following the greatest diplomat of the twentieth century.

Convergent growth has been breaking down for some years. Overlapping graphs have been replaced by a fractal pattern, in other words one with variable, shifting and overlapping geometries that are quick to form. It seems that there is no longer any peak on which to converge. Europe is undoubtedly in a frightening decline, militarily, in the first place, because it has not been able to transform the Franco-German armies and the armies that surrounded them into a new European army. From this viewpoint, the disarming of Germany, so strongly desired by the Soviet Union above all, for very obvious reasons, was disastrous, not merely for European world political hegemony, but also for European economic growth that was mutilated by the threatening yet formidable driving force of the German army for centuries and centuries even before German unification. Anyone who is old enough to have grown up in a time when good reading was important for personal development will remember Otto Brunner's thesis in his masterpiece entitled "Land and Lordship", which was that the formidable combination of force of arms and feudal land ownership laid the foundations of Prussian power in particular, but also that of the most powerful German states prior to unification. We could say that without a German army, Europe has lost its influence worldwide, whether we like it or not.

We have not been able to even attempt to overcome our poisonous dislike of the Fourth Reich in the interests of building a harmonious and united continental army, which might have delayed the global European decline that inevitably become irreversible after World War II. I have always believed it to be very telling that the only Armed Forces that did not withdraw from Berlin or Germany in the 1950s, as the French and British did, were the Soviet and North American forces. North America began its world deployment homogeneously in Asia as well, here too with the disarmament of Japan, despite the tremendous threat of communist revolution in China. The Korean War was not fought by the Japanese or the Europeans but only by English-speaking soldiers, first and foremost North Americans. This military decline has of course been masked for decades by the creation of NATO, but this was more a diplomatic than a military exercise, as has been made clear by the war in Libya: the intervention of the USA was decisive and that of the French, British and Italian troops was merely incidental.

This military rule is being redefined. This is because, despite the skirmishes that are still going on, the Soviet Union has collapsed and Putin's Russia is dangerously isolated from the West: less threatening. The increasingly evident North American disengagement from Europe is accompanied by economic downturn in Europe, which is also increasingly evident and worrisome, above all due to the population decline that is both the fruit and the cause of this decline. This has led to the emergence of fractal growth, in other words unequal growth that shows strong variables even within the same areas of growth.

The growth of Asia is impetuous and often overestimated because too little is known about it. Here, very different social and economic realities coexist with one another. We are left with the nub of the matter: nowadays, a divergence has come about instead of a convergence. If we look at things from a European viewpoint, in other words from the viewpoint of European shrinkage, this clearly diverges from the pattern of Asian growth. I prefer to talk about European divergence from trans-Pacific growth, in other words growth in the area that has the Pacific Realm at its heart and that has seen the United States perform a hegemonic function, unifying 800 million people in a trade treaty: from the Philippines to Burma, India, Vietnam, Mexico, Peru, Chile, New Zealand and ultimately Australia. The United States has drawn up a military treaty with these nations whose meaning is extremely clear, when we consider that China has been excluded from this major agreement.

European divergence from world growth emerges strikingly if we view it from the context of trans-Pacific indicators. But the most striking fractal pattern is that of the United States, whose fate is an enigma. During the current world economic crisis, the fate of North America also seems to be divergent. But as soon as we lift our heads from the statistical data and look at the power of attraction that the North American military and economic machine exercises over all the areas of new growth, we become less certain about that divergence. It is certainly a divergence with a variable geometry, involving military, technological, energy control and capability peaks that continue to advance over every area of new growth. If we go on to consider the role that the United States has again begun to exercise over the past 20 years—by no coincidence after the fall of the Soviet Union and in South America, where the Brazilian juggernaut is now definitely here to stay—we become increasingly uncertain of the North American decline.

What has changed is something more radical than the economy. It is the capability for strategic direction and hegemony: the Gulf and North African wars are a striking demonstration of this. Is this all about a striking lack of ability by a young president or something much deeper? This is the crucial question. This is the real danger facing the West and hence a threat to the whole world.

Emerge from the Crisis in Europe: Change Europe

In short, the world is changing, at an incredible pace. We need only look at what is happening in the capital market. The towering clouds of speculation always seemed invincible: and so they were for a long time. We all remember the 1990s, the Bank of England bled itself dry in an attempt to shore up the pound and to no avail: Soros made unprecedented gains. And the same thing happened with the Italian Lira: the "Ciampi-Amato"[1] devaluation leading to a swingeing overnight interest rate hike came about when the Bank of Italy lost control of events and its strategy of containment was overcome. Only the US Federal Reserve somehow managed to keep control of events… by going along with them. In short, the central banks were under attack.

Now the tide has turned in the USA, in Japan, in the United Kingdom, in Canada, in Brazil and in Mexico: the central banks are moving into the attack. They are following a strategy of subduing the clouds of speculation by issuing more money than those clouds can reach. A surprising change of tack and one that is also supported by revelations that fill with pride mavericks like myself, who objected to the slender evidence in papers suggesting a negative correlation between high public debt and low growth. These had no scientific basis. There were only a few of us: Krugman, Stiglitz, myself and a few others. Now the Director General of the International Monetary Fund, Ms. Lagarde, is slickly telling us that everything was a big mistake. Yet she fell for it too and on this slender

---

[1] On 11 July 1992, the Amato Government passed a financial stability decree-law worth 30,000 billion Lire that included a shocking provision—a 0.6 % one-off levy on bank accounts.

evidence justified the policy of austerity, destroying the physical stock of capital—companies. Not to mention destroying the people who made it possible for that stock to produce wealth—tens and tens of millions of whom are now unemployed in the OECD.

Now governments have taken back the sceptre of power: central bankers are toeing the line. The reason? Everybody is terrified by the unremitting global crisis. It is even sweeping towards Brazil, Russia and India, the famous BRICS saviours. Even China is slowing down. So we are printing money and introducing tax relief policies. In Europe, however, even though the crisis is beginning to affect Germany, nothing is moving. Draghi has been stopped in his tracks after his courageous and very useful attempts to circumvent the statute of the European Central Bank. Now everything has stopped. As far as growth is concerned: no one talks about Eurobonds anymore and it is taboo even to look at monetary and political–economic solidarity. In short, the world has set off at a tangent and Europe, by contrast, looks on. It is not moving.

The Nordic–Teutonic ice age is bringing about its deflationary effects: business margins are collapsing, prices are collapsing (hence deflation), employment is collapsing, fear and terror stalk the streets. A current of political and social destabilisation is beginning that is accelerating with violent shockwaves. And this is happening more than anywhere else in our own beleaguered Italy, which is on the brink of the abyss. Yet nothing changes. The State General Accounting Office, for example, is not answerable to Parliament, it is not even answerable to the Ministries of the Economy and Development. It is not answerable to anyone.

In Japan, they have dismissed the Governor of the Central Bank. In Italy, a bureaucracy that is answerable to a power—which is not even supranational in a political sense because it is merely a bureaucratic caste with European affiliations that are also bureaucratic—cannot even be challenged when it does everything to avoid returning money that the state owes to the companies that are our oxygen for survival. This is proof that the economy is dependent in everything and for everything on the underlying culture. We are in the grip of an all-too familiar form of Italian fundamentalism: the important thing is not to win but to stop another from winning, even if this means death and destruction.

The interest groups now in power in Germany and Northern Europe are admittedly intent on domination, but whether we like it or not their long-term plan is lucid and always pursued in accordance with a deep-seated historical tradition that we can challenge but not ignore. With us, it is different: our economy is controlled by a power caste currently defending a policy of austerity that is beginning even in Europe to be defined as suicidal and there is a commitment to re-negotiate. It is effectively a weapon of mass destruction: we need only think of the "stability pact". Stability of what? In short, the house is burning down and its guardians are preventing the firemen from entering, thinking only of saving themselves. I would not like to have to resort to asking President Giorgio Napolitano to let the firemen into our own house.

We have no time to lose. We need to take action in Italy as well as in Europe to pave the way for emergence from the crisis. Unemployment has reached levels that, as the Governor of the Bank of Italy reminded us, threaten social cohesion. In other words, to put it a little less euphemistically, a great mass of suffering and danger to social order. The government must continue to challenge European austerity and establish itself as a spearhead for all those who wish to break the ice of the tundra that threatens to melt and sink us. What should we do? It is complicated, but there is a way.

On the one hand, we need to reassure the financial and pseudo-technocratic European–Teutonic oligopoly that we want to reduce waste by ultimately securitising public property owned by state and local authorities. One decisive action would be to launch a forced loan by offering government bonds, forcing those with incomes of over €200,000 to invest an amount equivalent to 0.5 % of their assets in order to disguise pseudo-occult capital as a loan for the country that will not scare anyone. This would enable us to slash company and employment taxes. In this context, even working with cash surpluses, we could finance a working plan based on the principle that job creation is not achieved by liberalising the labour market, but by investing in key areas for growth, such as infrastructure, new 3-D technologies and the mechatronics clusters that are essential to the life of our more advanced small- and medium-sized enterprises. Am I thinking of a new IRI?[2] No. We should not create hospitals to save the lives of ailing companies. Investment creates profit and employment, and not the other way round. And so the state must again become an entrepreneur based on the historical model introduced by ENI, but with the legal form of a British trust and not that of a managing entity. In other words, there should be no Board of Directors, but single serving directors. This needs to be done soon because the world situation is not

---

[2]IRI, Istituto per la Ricostruzione Industriale (Institute for Industrial Reconstruction), was an Italian public holding company established in 1933 by the Fascist regime to rescue, restructure and finance banks and private companies that went bankrupt during the Great Depression. After the Second World War, IRI played a pivotal role in the Italian economic miracle of the 1950s and 1960s. It was dissolved in 2000.

favourable. Because of this, it is really wrong to think that we can emerge from the crisis quickly, especially if the focus is on structural defects.

The warning signs are beginning to mount. I have already pointed out one fact that has not yet gained the notice it deserves: the recent appointment of the Brazilian career diplomat Roberto Carvalho de Azevêdoas the head of the WTO, the organisation that has as its goal the development of world trade. Brazil did not hesitate to conduct a premeditated currency war and is also pursuing a form of targeted protectionism aimed at supporting domestic industries and agricultural production based on the economic policy chosen by the government. As we know, these are the principles followed in one way or another, with slight variations, by all the "BRICS" countries (Brazil, India, China, Russia and South Africa) despite the military and financial efforts that the USA in particular set in motion to change its trade policy. For this reason, it is very likely that the trend that has emerged over the past 10 years of pursuing bilateral instead of multilateral trade agreements will continue, with inevitable negative consequences on world trade.

The second consequence will be that, as has been happening for some time in Europe with regard to austerity, the theory of full-blown globalisation will give way to a form of globalisation that is more tempered with regard to free trade with consequent falls in world trade. The consequences on the European economy will be profound. The ideology suggesting that only exporting countries can grow will be faced with its first difficulties, and this is also revealed by information on the future German economic situation that is really disturbing. We now lack global demand, in other words internal markets, and we can also expect a fall in international demand, with a reduction in export areas and increasing difficulty in carving out new export niches. Will Europe continue to stand by and watch? We will act immediately, regardless.

The merciless newsletters from the Bank of Italy leave no room for doubt: public debt continues to increase without economic growth. Quite the opposite, it is growing at a time of depression, of deflation. The sum amounts to €2,034,725 billion, surpassing every historical record and destroying the illusions of those who support the austerity policy. This increase continues, month by month, unstoppably. Above all—and herein lies the problem—it is not offset by a rebalancing of expenditure. In other words, central government departments continue to show an increase in expenditure well above that of the local authorities that really have nothing more to spend due to the nooses we have put around the necks of local administrators. Despite this, tax revenues have increased slightly by 0.79 % compared to the same quarter of 2012. All this is very difficult to take in at first sight: tax revenues rise but cannot offset the increase in debt that has become an insurmountable and unstoppable force. There is something more at play here than the simple but infernal debt/GDP ratio. Few people know that a large proportion of the increase in debt now comes directly from our European commitments, in other words from the "common" projects that we share with Europe, such as the European Stability Mechanism and the European Financial Stability Facility. Paradoxically, both of these projects should pave the way for the mutualisation of debt and harmonisation of the financial networks towards which Europe has been working for years. For now, these mutual actions have cost us €43 billion, which we pay in monthly instalments. The idea is that these funds should act as life rafts for countries in difficulty. This concept of mutuality naturally applies only to the collection of capital when the harvest is home. But as Cyprus has shown us, it does not apply when it comes to distributing hay to the sheep grazing on the green meadows of Europe because Germany and the Nordic states are firmly opposed to this mutualisation. In the meantime, though, we continue to harvest the hay. We will see what can be done with it, despite the fact that public debt in southern European countries is growing steadily and no one is benefiting from these efforts due to the asymmetries of power revealed in this way.

The problem is worsening, and at first sight, it is incomprehensible if we consider that this increase in debt, or rather debts, coincides with a fall in inflation that is generalised and does affect not only the energy assets that have been forced into temporary shrinkage by the authorities, but also consumer goods and many manufactured items as well as many intermediate products. In short, debt increases because the Italian economy is locked into a deep deflation marked by a fall in consumption, production and business margins. These effects are not compensated for by the persistently good performances that continue to be shown by exporting countries. But not everyone can export and global demand and therefore the internal market always have the last word when it comes to making a judgement about an economy. In short, the path of growth is narrowing.

Despite the deflationary fall, the state must continue to spend to overcome the failures of our government. In this critical situation, Prime Minister Letta acted like a European statesman with double derailment of the two golden rules demanded of Europe (removing expenditure for infrastructure and social cohesion from the deficit). But his sudden fall, with a desertion reminiscent of the situation in Australia, in other words one that followed the pattern of a struggle within the ruling party as happened in the Labour Party of Rudd and Gillard, led to the epiphenomenon of the USA removing their support for a group of political leaders who ultimately proved themselves too weak in the face of the German *diktat*. When Letta's opposition for certain anti-deflationary ECB proposals (that were in all cases only heralded, in truth, by its President, who is a polished PR performer) came to light, this proved fatal for the Letta-Alfano government. After that, it only remained to remove the government. This was deftly done by the Italian President of the Republic who unsurprisingly received a private visit a few short months later from Queen Elizabeth, symbolic holder of effective British situational power with very deep and esoteric origins.

A fight within the Democratic Party then ultimately led to the Renzi government and takes us back to the starting point of our reflections on Italy and the world and on the world and Italy. This is incidentally also an outstanding case study on the problem of the relationship between nation and internationalisation.

We are left with one problem: reassuring the international financial oligopoly that our debt can be not eliminated, of course, but at least monitored for the purposes of growth without further uncertainties.

We are faced with two paths. The first is to follow the wind of change that is sweeping through Europe from the USA and Japan and prompts the thought that under these conditions an increase in debt reflects the commitments of an asymmetrical Europe as well as the absence of growth and that a little more debt will not therefore make much difference because, this should be stressed, this increase is aimed at stimulating demand and kick-starting production. I repeat: kick-starting production, in other words exempting capitalist labour and profit from taxation and investing in public works, particularly to revive the building industry and support manufacturing. Growth will come and we will deal with debt later.

At the same time, however, we must reassure the still very strong supporters of the austerity policy that the very worst catastrophes will come about if debt is not reduced, even if only nominally. We can keep them happy. We have entire libraries filled with plans, projects, theories and studies. In that case, let us begin to securitise the property of state and local authorities and draw up plans to cut costs that are not justifiable. What happened to our good intentions about standard costs? It was the best idea put forward by those noble proponents of fiscal federalism. The kleptocratic potential of the Italian economy and society would of course be reduced, just as the regulated and controlled sale of property would put an end to a situation where towns are full of abandoned buildings whilst satellite towns grow up with no concern for proper town planning and the demand for housing would be relieved. We would kill two birds with one stone: restart growth in the building sector with its formidable knock-on effects and give back a little certainty to the economy as a whole and thus to Italian families. Come on, dear friends of the government: Italy expects this of you.

A government announces, in muted tones, a U-turn on all its economic policy of recent years, a very bold change of direction with nothing to shout about and proclaim. And this would not have been possible in any case because the array of forces supporting the new government is very similar to that of the Monti government.

But the politics are quite different: the sound of the politics that we are finally once again hearing in Parliament has a harmonious note. Herein lies the triumph of a political as opposed to a technocratic choice, which turns into economic policy with its attendant technical expertise and skills, a 180° turn, not yet 360°, but we are not complaining. This is a hard blow for the supporters of Nordic–Teutonic austerity and of subordination to theories that have brought the world to the brink of the precipice—which have all now turned out to be wrong! Enrico Letta, who was still Prime Minister at that time, did not dwell on this in his inaugural address. Great intelligence must be not only tactical, but strategic if we want peace to persist and consolidate. There is no need to cry over spilt milk in this nicely judged return to a style of pure politics where what matters is the execution of programmes and their implementation, not going around yelling that you are right and everyone else is wrong.

Of course, above everything, we are now seeing a different view of the relationship with Europe that is the diametric opposite to that of Monti et al. But this does not need saying. We need to act. We are indeed confident that the much-vaunted tax relief will come about: do away with IMU municipal taxation on the first home, do away with unfair taxation destroying the value of employment and work itself as well as of businesses and workers—and no more increase in VAT, but guarantee structured and targeted tax relief to ensure the recovery of the core building industry. To those who question how to finance these measures, the answer is implicit. Here too, there is no need to proclaim it to the four winds: the stability pact will be re-negotiated for local authorities as well as for the whole of Italy. In other words, the fiscal compact will be re-negotiated: apart from anything else, Spain has already paved the way. The French and Germans, whose polemic has been defused by a foundering Hollande, will find Italy a restorative tonic that should not humiliate Germany but bring it back to reason; otherwise, the outcome will be the destruction of the European productive system, including that of Germany itself.

At long last, Italy has acquired a European credibility that it formerly lacked because what credibility it had was not political but achieved by technicians working in the service of politics. And decision-makers are not made in a day, despite what long-winded media trickery would have you believe. Now, however, Italy has full and acknowledged European political credibility: we will negotiate as equals, not between masters and subordinates. The Matteo Renzi-led government that has replaced Letta is continuing this policy with even more momentum. Europe's variable geometry will change. We will break through the 3 % deficit ceiling and we will stop fetishising debt.

Foreign investors are helping us, and they will help us more and more, confirming the soundness of the ideas put forward by we poor scholars with our heads forever in our books who maintained that, even for financial oligopolies, the problem is never sovereign debt but growth: in other words, the sheep should never be killed; if anything it should be sheared... and the only thing that kills is failure to grow and not debt. Japan and the USA have taught us this. Now we come to the bravest part of the programme, which will defeat the Jonahs of posterity once and for all: the minimum wage or basic income, call it what you will; funding income support systems for those who have lost their jobs and solving the problem of older redundant workers, who were plunged into a limbo of despair by the shameful inability of incompetent technocrats with a lack of any sense of justice that I found terrifying.

Economic policy is back in the arena. It is still tip-toeing about, but it is back. The thoughts of the great Federico Caffè, who is all too often overlooked, and the Keynesian Beniamino Andreatta are appearing over the horizon: masters, great role models. We are beginning to breathe again. We may be about to see a new era of dignity and sensitivity for work, businesses, artisans, traders, private and public sector employees. This illustrates how good it is to leave behind hate campaigns and return to politics. Without politics, economy is just another technique, not merely sad but one that can inflict pain and destruction. Now we must rebuild. We will make it together.

The great theme of today and tomorrow, of the new Italian government and the Eurozone, is and will be that of job creation. To be more specific, I would like to make it clear that it will not be about the clichéd old "labour market": instead, it will be about the simpler and more understandable concept of job creation. We must be realistic: creating jobs means stimulating new investment because only investment creates jobs. This goal must become the vocation of economists as well as that of politicians. An economy is not merely fair but good—in other words it works well—if it tends to full employment. Today's unemployment figures, on the other hand, make gruesome reading. They are even worse if you look at youth employment. They are worrying for Southern Europe, led by Spain, and for continental Europe, with record figures for France. But they are bad even for Germany which, due to the fact that years ago it created two employment markets with profoundly unequal wage levels, is also beginning to have problems of internal demand and has therefore seen its growth forecasts drop alarmingly with a consequent hike in unemployment rates.

In short, we must look reality in the face: attempts to create employment by merely liberalising the labour market, in other words by allowing precarious employment on a generalised basis, have resulted in resounding failures. Of course, the social consequences have been more or less severe according to whether the liberalisation of temporary contracts is or is not accompanied by reasonable tax relief on employers but above all support systems for those who had to submit to flexible working conditions yet without ever slipping through the social and contribution support network that changed fixed-term employment into "flexicurity". In other words, they were and are accompanied by an extensive and safe support network between one job and the next that is typical, for example, of the Dutch jobseekers system.

In countries such as Italy, on the other hand, where a culture of precarious work has taken root in the absence of a social security cushion, fixed-term employment has become insecure precarious employment with severe demographic and social consequences. Furthermore, for employers too, this has been simultaneously accompanied by a policy of taxing short-term contracts that reveals an anthropological misunderstanding of the social role of an employer. An entirely opposite, negative anthropological view is thus established of a person who takes pleasure in sacking people and not hiring people and naturally tending to deception and fraud even when he deigns to do so.

This is the worst possible attitude to managing employment issues. In the first place, no jobs will ever be created like this. Everything about it is wrong. We must start from a positive business anthropology and above all we must encourage flexicurity without burdening employers but by expanding public expenditure on social safety nets, calling for the European "golden rule", in other words excluding from the deficit calculation expenditure on social cohesion as well as expenditure on infrastructure. We need to encourage apprenticeships and all ways of integrating young people in work, adjusting the turnover according to the numbers who are about to reach retirement age. This is the approach adopted in the important Chemists' contract[3] signed in 2013, which introduces innovative ideas on the topic of job creation that have not attracted the attention they deserve.

In short, we need to massively promote investment and in order to do this we must use all possible resources in the field of economic policy. Turkey, for example, did so by supporting recruitment through allocating part of the state budget

---

[3]In Italy, collective agreements are negotiated at national level and apply for categories of employers (industrial plants, hotels, airlines, etc.). Here, reference is made to the chemists collective agreement signed in 2013.

for tax relief on contributions for new employees and shouldering charges for part of the new wage bill, considering it a necessary sacrifice for creating new employment. Must we look outside Europe to see hopes rekindle? Maybe. We must do everything we can, not only for Italy to find peace again but also to make it a land that sees growth, through a new economic policy, employment, work. This is the only way we will beat the crisis.

The Italian government is faced with a terrible trial. It has before it two completely different paths that amount to a genuine crossroads. One approach could be to chip away at the crisis at all possible points of attack, starting at a national level, fighting revenue and waste. The theoretical and practical justification for this strategy is that certain existing resources that could be used to encourage domestic demand and investment are instead wasted to benefit powerful groups, who squander public and private assets by feeding legal and illegal cartels to the detriment of capitalist profit and employment, the only real drivers of long-term growth and job creation. This is a debate that exercised the most brilliant economic minds of the day in the 1970s, including Sylos Labini, Federico Caffè and Claudio Napoleoni. It found a sympathetic ear in Andreatta—who acted as a bridge between these worlds—in Giorgio Amendola and in Ugo La Malfa, as well as, naturally, in Guido Carli and Paolo Savona.

The problems of today are the same as they were then: how to find resources to lower taxes on consumption and on capital income that produce growth and feed domestic demand? (We cannot live on exports alone!) We can find them by applying standard costs, in other words not by applying the linear costs that depress the GDP and mean it does not grow and are the dark side of austerity, but by breaking the kleptocratic covenant between local politicians funded by the companies they assist that survive due to the resources the same politicians ensure these companies receive, thus destroying the legal unity of the state and institutional and moral fairness. From this point of view, the country is disintegrating. Italy's own Premier must spearhead a political and cultural movement to break up these revenue streams and set himself up as a politician who is able to do what the technical governments have not managed to do and will never be able to do.

The very issue of privatisation should also be viewed in this light: do not sell off the crown jewels but open the doors to new investments and new players that we can work with in the new, larger companies that will be able to emerge due to this injection of capital and innovatory managerial energy. Let us not beat about the bush. Wherever politics is pursued through democratic institutionalisation, in other words through a battle that is not waged between enemies armed against one another but between opponents, this way of doing politics is the constitutional essence of any coalition government. Let us hope that all possible reform is carried out in Italy in accordance with the approach I propose here, but we should not forget that the real battle must be fought in Europe. It is a very difficult struggle and we must make haste. Time may already have run out, but it is still worth trying.

Europe is declining first of all internationally, with the proven international rift that the inter-Islamic wars are now laying bare with the terrible transatlantic split between the United Kingdom and the USA. This cannot be patched up by the French posturing as a beneficent imperial power, but one without ideas and without resources. After the failure that was made manifest when it could not prevent the genocidal Balkan wars, the Gulf–North African wars are really putting Europe in check.

This particular chess match is even more risky because the USA is at a major cultural and strategic impasse and has shown itself incapable of exercising world hegemony (not dominion, God forbid, those days are past!). Without that hegemony the world is a sick place.

In this context, the scale of the European economic crisis has become critical. Europe is indeed declining economically. Austerity is beginning to have consequences similar to those of a lost war. The destruction of Europe's industrial heritage continues and is not counterbalanced by the clinging on (clinging on, please note, not growth!) of Germany's manufacturing machine. As far as services are concerned, too, we are also at a standstill, against a backdrop of falling margins. The telecommunication sector is a good example: Vodafone and Verizon are growing and restructuring, but in the USA, whilst Europe is becoming their hunting ground for both landlines and mobile phones. And the world of information technology has not thrown up one idea, a single idea, for years. For this reason, instead of austerity, we need the opposite: a Marshall Plan for Europe that stops the deflationary spiral and reforms the ECB, making it similar to the North American FED, breathing new life into private and public investments, dismantling the Maastricht Treaty and the crazy and ill-thought through constraints that arise out of it. We will keep the Euro, of course, but in a reformed institutional context. This must be our clarion cry. The alternative is the desert and fratricidal strife.

GPSR Compliance
The European Union's (EU) General Product Safety Regulation (GPSR) is a set of rules that requires consumer products to be safe and our obligations to ensure this.

If you have any concerns about our products, you can contact us on

ProductSafety@springernature.com

In case Publisher is established outside the EU, the EU authorized representative is:

Springer Nature Customer Service Center GmbH
Europaplatz 3
69115 Heidelberg, Germany

www.ingramcontent.com/pod-product-compliance
Lightning Source LLC
LaVergne TN
LVHW040743250326
834688LV00031B/416